THE A-Z OF
FANTASY FOOTBALL

THE GAFFER TAPES

PRESENTS

THE A-Z OF
FANTASY
F⚽⚽TBALL

A HILARIOUS GUIDE
FILLED WITH ANECDOTES
AND EXPERT ADVICE

TOM HOLMES, CRAIG HAZELL
AND ASH KERNSWORTH

First published by Pitch Publishing, 2019

Pitch Publishing
A2 Yeoman Gate
Yeoman Way
Worthing
Sussex
BN13 3QZ
www.pitchpublishing.co.uk
info@pitchpublishing.co.uk

A CIP catalogue record is available for this book
from the British Library.

ISBN 978 1 78531 506 0

Typesetting and origination by Pitch Publishing

Printed and bound in the UK by TJ International, Padstow, Cornwall

Contents

Foreword

I'LL be honest, I have no idea why I've been asked to do this foreword.

I don't like fantasy football – I don't even like football. I do, however, like fantasies: for example, chocolate covered boobies or a world without football.

In fact I don't actually know if I know what fantasy football is. My friends from *The Gaffer Tapes* asked me to do this and I said yes because I always pretend to listen to their podcast but never actually have and that makes me feel bad. I'm writing this to make myself feel better for all the lies and you know what? It's working. I'm such a great guy.

I used to love pretending to like football. It was around the same time I was pretending to like olives. I pretended to support Liverpool and I pretended to cry when they lost in the FA Cup Final to Manchester United with a late goal from some guy who I can't be bothered to google. I don't think I was ever angry enough to like it. Football fans seem so angry. Even when they win they are aggressively happy.

Last summer, when England outperformed everyone's low expectations, I saw a street taken over with white shirts where chairs and tables were thrown and the riot police were called. That was when we won. During the madness, I saw a man steal a bike, holding it aloft while singing 'it's coming home! It's coming home!' I'm glad something did because the person who owned that bike didn't.

Ok, for the sake of this book let me try and be more positive. I do like three things about football.

I like that the goalkeepers (is that one word or two?), are not allowed to celebrate when they do a good save, even though technically it's as good as a goal. So instead, knowing everyone is looking at them, they hold the ball and shout and point.

I also like the singing aspect. Somehow everyone learns the words without a hymn sheet being handed out, which I find wonderfully impressive.

Finally, I like it when the fans see themselves on the big screen and just as they get excited the camera switches to someone fresh. I think being the man in control of that has one of the finest jobs available, better than a stand-up comedian or professional foreword writer.

I hope you enjoy this book more than I like football. I think you will. I've read it and its great. Ok, I haven't read it, but I promise to read it one day guys, while simultaneously listening to your shitty podcast.

I'm off to scour the internet for chocolate covered boobies. Byeeee

Joel Dommett

Introduction

I F we had to describe fantasy football to an alien, we wouldn't, we'd be far too busy worrying about where he was going to put his massive bony finger. We'd also be wanting to engage the little fella in more beneficial, existential conversation than explaining bonus points, what a wildcard was and when was the best time to use it. We'd want to know if the alien race really *were* behind the construction of the pyramids, if the *Men in Black* movie franchise is at all realistic, and if Mesut Özil is actually one of them. Come on, look at the eyes! If, after a few hours, the alien *still* wanted to know the ins and outs of fantasy football, then we'd probably have to indulge him. It's only polite, innit? So, take a seat, put up a tentacle and let *The Gaffer Tapes* walk you through the unique pastime that is 'the game of the beautiful game'.

Unfortunately, fantasy football in the United Kingdom is dwarfed by its transatlantic cousin. The NFL is big business, and fantasy football out in the States is equally as colossal; there's a disgusting amount of money to be made in and around American fantasy football. Regrettably, that's not the case with our fantasy football (or *proper* fantasy football, as we like to refer to it) because if there was we'd be bloody rolling in it, mate. In fact, five years ago, when we first started recording our podcast, we were inundated with questions regarding the American game, because people were under the misconception that we were an NFL show. Who to pick at quarterback? What guy to go with in the flex? Do you think he'll be found guilty? At first we used to correct them as well as telling them that by 'fantasy football' they mean 'fantasy soccer' and by 'fantasy soccer' they mean 'fantasy football', the word-stealing, language-butchering, overweight hicks. After a few months of the NFL questions, however, we gave up and just started offering advice. *Yeah, pick Tom Brady, he's got lovely legs. Flex is a tough call, maybe go with Smithson, he will touchdown that pigskin right in their bloody endzone. He's definitely guilty.*

The Gaffer Tapes have grown and evolved with the game of (proper) fantasy football; from recording our ramblings on an iPhone to about 12 listeners, to being downloaded millions of times in over 50 countries. We've written about it for the likes of the SPORTbible and talked about it on TalkSPORT radio, or, to be more specific, we were called 'nerds' by the hosts while talking about it on TalkSPORT radio. We've dreamt about it, lived it, breathed it, loved it and hated it, all in equal measures. It's got to the stage where we can't look at cold temperatures on a weather map without it bringing back memories of bad fantasy football scores of the past, or hear a pilot introduce himself and the first officer without thinking about that weekend's line-up announcements. And god forbid when someone tells me their phone number and it ends in 433. Because that's the problem – fantasy football warps how you look at the world and how much you actually enjoy playing the game. For us, being involved in a full-time capacity for so long means that playing fantasy football has become somewhat of a busman's holiday and has kind of ruined it a little bit. Like how working at the Mars factory ruins chocolate or working at Sports Direct really puts you off massive mugs … but that's probably no way to talk about Mike Ashley.

Ever since you first shouted at a manager from the stands or from the other side of a television screen, you became a fantasy football manager. You may not have started playing the actual game of fantasy football until years later, but from that first yell of frustration, you knew what needed to be done – you knew you could do a better job. Fantasy football is your chance to be that football manager. Personally, we think that being a fantasy football manager is actually more difficult and a hell of a lot less rewarding than managing a real team. Think about it, you're on your own in fantasy football, you don't have a team of coaching staff behind you, assisting you with tactics and formation, feeding you information on players' fitness levels and telling you how brilliant you are constantly. Nope, it's just you and your team.

Will we be able to enhance and nurture your inner football manager? Yeah, we'd like to think so. Will the pages of this book help you realise your full potential, impart some high-level wisdom which will tip the balance of the universe and transform you into one of the greatest fantasy football managers of all time? No. No, we probably won't. But will we talk you through what a ball-ache it can be and laugh at some people who are even worse at it than you? Oh yes. Don't get us wrong, there will be some tips and fantasy discussion that should assist you on your fantasy footballing journey, and some comical anecdotes and observations that will keep you laughing if they don't. We may not help you win the whole of fantasy football, but we'll have a bloody good go at helping you beat your mates, and that's the most important thing, right?

We've been involved in fantasy football for years and as a result have seen our own fair share of highs and lows, from top-100 overall finishes to drunken transfers that resulted in losing mini-leagues. We'll be pouring everything we have in our huge, swollen kit bags on to these pages, in what we are certain will be the definitive guide to fantasy football. We delve into the time-wasting, procrastinating and commiserating, we scrutinise the forfeits, formations and 'for Christ's sakes!' We look at stories of misfortune, mistakes and miracles, and there's insight into the history, heroes and heresy of fantasy football. We talk to current professional footballers about their teams, who they pick, who they refuse to include and whether they're vain enough to select themselves. There's insight from celebrities, presenters and comedians who sat down with us and made us feel a lot better about the amount of time *we* spend on fantasy football, knowing that successful public figures (people with actual 'lives') do it too.

There's something for everyone within. Whether you've played fantasy football before, you're interested in giving it a go in the future, or just like hearing stories of people being forced to walk through the streets naked as a punishment. Regardless of whether you're the sort of fantasy football manager who spends more time looking at colour-coded spreadsheets than in the shower, or the sort who forgets his password by the third week and doesn't really care, this guide is for you. If, however, you are an aforementioned alien being, then welcome to Earth and have a read of the book while you're here. Sorry we've left the place in a bit of a state and that it's all knoheads in charge. If you're looking for anyone to take back with you to your spaceship and probe, then we would like to recommend a lovely little chap called Sepp Blatter; absolutely great bloke and a perfect representation of human life, plus he loves a backhander – if you know what I mean. Don't worry about returning him.

A Brief History of Fantasy Football

AS your average fantasy football boffin tinkers with his line-up on his app, scrolls through the research blogs on his Mac to the backdrop of one of 3,000 fantasy podcasts blaring through his Google Home device, it's hard to believe fantasy football even existed before the internet. He declined to comment but we're pretty sure Tim Berners Lee didn't have middle-aged men in their pants frantically hunting for West Bromwich Albion's injury list when he invented the World Wide Web. Then again, he didn't envisage ratemypoo.com either and that remains a classic. The fact remains, though, that there's a generation (or two) of football fans who don't remember the analogue version of the game we all love to hate.

Way back before the Premier League became the hook to hang your fantasy football on, there was a weird play-by-mail service that used to advertise in the back of football magazines and therein lies my first encounter with the world's nerdiest hobby. Right between the penis pumps and the sex lines lay the tiny font asking if you wanted to become a football manager. It speaks to my depressing realism that even at 11 I knew my chances of becoming a football manager far outweighed any success I would have on a sex line, so I decided to take them up on their offer of your 'first week free'. Knowing I could never use my home phone, as it sat in the hallway and my dad could read an itemised bill like Johnny 5 in *Short Circuit*, I snuck into the headmaster's office at school and phoned the number, putting on a deep voice to give over my details. If this is how nervous I was to play postal fantasy football, Jesus knows how I'd have coped trying to order the penis pump. One week later I received a letter with about 73 unnecessary pieces of paper that included my squad (a random list of 20 players from around the world) and a match report from my first game. It then dawned on me: this was just some guy in his bedroom writing out 15-page match reports from a fictional football match, between fictional teams and fictional players. In fact, the only thing that was real was the wasted hours and the disappointment of his parents. To play a second game week, you had to send a cheque for £1.99 and to make transfers you needed to call other managers from the league and discuss it with them. The shame of it! Safe to say, I did not invest that two quid and the only purpose play-by-mail served me was that I went through a phase of signing up on my friends' dads' behalves because the confusion it would cause them amused me.

Like cutting off people's heads when taking a photo on a disposable camera, I never saw the punchline but I enjoyed it nonetheless. The fact that there was a subculture of people whose highlight of the week was reading football fan fiction proved that there was an appetite for creating a game within a game. After all, fantasy football was, and still is, a way for people to love the sport while being utterly useless at it. No different to looking at houses you can't afford on Zoopla, girls you can't date on Tinder or going to houses on Zoopla where that girl on Tinder lives. It's all escapism and another way to fanaticise about football, just like kids do now with Instagram and we did then with Panini stickers. Thankfully, someone had the bright idea to use actual football instead of some sort of cosplay hybrid, and the play-by-mail game died. But there isn't a day goes by when I don't think about it.

The factual answer to who is the man behind fantasy football, which you can regurgitate to your mates down the pub, is that Italian journalist Riccardo Albini is widely considered as the inventor of fantasy football outside America, or the 'Hand of Godfather' if you want to ensure your mates don't ask you this question again. Albini adopted the stats from baseball in the late 80s and worked out a way to accommodate 'soccer' in the already huge fantasy market in America, where they had been playing since the 1960s. And so, FantaCalcio was born. The first tournaments were played during the 1988 European Championships, and in 1990 Albini published *Serie A – Fantacalcio,* which basically acted as the server to the game. One can only hope that the first-ever fantasy football team was called 'The Albini Babies'. And if you want to be meta and post that Kermit drinking tea meme you're so desperately keen to use, you should think about calling yours that too next season and wait for the opportunity to be smug when told it's a shit name. Albini would spend his lunch breaks in Milan putting together the game and it seems only fitting that he has since vicariously occupied millions of lunch breaks ever since. It wasn't until *La Gazzetta* approached the inventor in 1994 that it became a national game and the version we now know. The original game used an auction system where all league members would bid for their squad for the season, which obviously needed modifying in order to be played by millions. Talking of millions, you'd think Albini would be rolling in it right? Wrong. He never really found an effective way of monetising it (a bit like podcasting), and without the foresight of the scale of it now he never really made anything off the back of changing our Saturday mornings forever. As an interesting footnote, Riccardo Albini was also responsible for bringing Sudoku to Europe in 2005, and you have to wonder whether the guy was just intent on pissing us all off one way or another. Glad he's not filthy rich now, aren't you?

A guy called Andrew Wainstein brought the game to the UK with Fantasy League, who still run the data for various newspapers as well as the original auction version of the game that most non-fantasy playing folk aren't au fait with. The game itself is actually a lot more enjoyable than the one we all know but can only be played with you and about nine mates, which doesn't make anyone any money, and by anyone we mean Rupert Murdoch. Honourably, you can still find Wainstein hosting auctions down the pub for Fantasy League members who still choose the purest form of the game. It's part of his job. He isn't just walking round approaching groups halfway through a quiz, shouting at them that he used to be a contender. The way it works is quite simple. The guy running the league introduces the players and the league members bid on him just like they do on *Bargain Hunt* on the telly. Whether you spend £40m of your £100m on Harry Kane early doors is up to you, or you could sit tight and watch other people blow their load on unproven new signings. You've just spotted the flaw in the game, haven't you? To do it properly, you have to introduce every potential player to the auction. What starts as an adrenaline rush of throwing fictional money into the air ends up like the opening scenes in *Ferris Bueller's Day Off*. Phil Jones? Phil Jones? Anyone? Anyone? A science teacher at my school took the questionable decision to run an auction league during the 1993/94 season, and, while a group of schoolboys being auctioned by their teacher sounds more like the last scene in *Taken*, it really was all above board. Although, looking back I wonder if it was some form of community service. I entered a team with my best mate Baz Barrett (sounds fictional: isn't), and Mr Nagel-Smith (sounds utterly implausible: honestly isn't) acted as league commissioner. By 3pm every Friday you had to have your line-ups in his pigeon hole to ensure your scores counted. The problem was, and I imagine *is,* that the auction remains the most fun part of it and the inability to tinker with your team is a huge downside to the game. It wasn't until Wainstein flogged the concept to national newspapers that it became something you could play on a grander scale and not just in your creepy science teacher's bedroom.

That's where this story starts for most of us as *The Telegraph* used Fantasy League to run their game in the mid-90s and, along with that week's episode of *Friends* and mad cow disease, it suddenly became water cooler chat in the office. I used to look forward to the first edition of the season, laying out the double-page spread from *The Telegraph*, calculator in hand, assembling a team of 11 heroes that would have to endure the entire season no matter what. *The Sun* did fantasy football too, but *their* double-page spreads didn't have the 13-year-old me reaching for my calculator. Back then, if Neil Ruddock broke his leg in a season opener then tough luck. Gutted, mate. He was yours for the season. Long before squad rotation, in a time when the word dogging innocently still involved Labradors, fantasy football still made up autumnal optimism and weekend regrets. Since then, it has evolved into a conundrum of wildcards and chips drizzled over a bed of double-game weeks and captaincy decisions. And if you still have Neil Ruddock's shattered fibula in your end-of-season team then you only have yourself to blame. Footnote, 'Neil Ruddock's Shattered Fibula' is an excellent fantasy football team name and in a way this book has already repaid itself in kind. For many, though, those early days of running your fingers through the ink of *The Telegraph* sports pages really *were* fantasy football. While the intention was for you to pick your 11 and then use the premium phone line to check scores and replace players throughout the season, I don't know a single person who fell for that nonsense. Speaking from experience, as a guy who went into my parents' room at 8am to ask the bill payer's permission to enter a competition on *Live & Kicking* to win an NBA Jam arcade machine, it was not a conversation I wanted to have again. Better still, my dad scoffed at the idea of joining their league at all and insisted on running the work league manually. He would create a full database for every person's squad and insert the scores by hand into a spreadsheet that calculated scores for the whole league. I don't think I had an appreciation until right now for how much time that must have taken and for just how deeply unhappy he must have been. Plus, the last thing he needed after spending all week doing that was me waking him up at 8am on a Saturday with the house phone in one hand, a copy of *The Sun* in the other, in my Batman pyjamas.

Imagine having to wait a whole week just to read your players' scores in the newspaper. Now imagine that you can't even see how your mates did because you can't click on their team and have no idea who they have in their side. Then imagine that all this information comes in a fucking broadsheet newspaper. Do you know how hard it is to spend your lunch break reading a broadsheet newspaper as a 12-year-old kid without getting the shit kicked out of you? You may as well wear a monocle and call your teacher Mum. Yet somehow, this game still gripped millions of people and we're still here 25 years later.

That is, of course, in no small part thanks to Messrs Baddiel and Skinner. Fantasy football became this zeitgeisty pop culture phenomenon and the BBC acted quickly to attach two football-loving comedians to become the face of it. Dominik Diamond of *GamesMaster* fame on Channel 4 had a cult hit radio show on 5 Live and it paved the way for Baddiel and Skinner to do their thing. *Fantasy Football League* became a show kids watched with their dads, understanding half the jokes and spawning a machine gun of catchphrases, all the while ruining Jason Lee's career. When you look at it now, it had absolutely nothing to do with fantasy football. Celebrities would come on and show you their team and then the other 59 minutes were filled with sketches and comedy and we bloody loved it. Any fantasy footy info came through the medium of 'Statto', aka Angus Loughran, who inexplicably wore pyjamas and a dressing gown as he gave useful tips. Although, in an age where assists weren't acknowledged, wildcards didn't exist and transfers cost you a phone call, it's hard to know exactly what insight Statto could actually give you. His real genius came in betting tips and an incredible memory for all things sport, so it often felt a bit unfair that his role was basically to get the piss ripped out of him by the hosts. Loughran's love of logistics and numbers did get him some karmic justice in the end though, as he was one of the original investors in OPTA, which sold for £47m in 2013.

That's better than constant royalties from the nation's best-loved football anthem right? RIGHT?! Well no, of course not. Statto was declared bankrupt in 2008, but come on, give the man a line in the song!

Fantasy Football League did leave us with a brilliantly awful piece of fantasy footy history as well as its iconic status as one of the best comedy programmes of the 90s, and that was with the official board game. Back in the 90s, everything had a board game. Some classics that are definitely worth tracking down were Noel's House Party, complete with a grab a grand box, Jim Davidson's Big Break, which was essentially a small snooker table, and The Crystal Maze, which was always going to struggle to successfully replicate the high-budget, physical game show we all knew and loved. It didn't even come with a sarcastic bald man or anything. Fantasy Manager was outrageously complicated and time-consuming to play, and as it was based entirely on the stats from the actual 93/94 season it could only really be played once. It came armed with a *Back to the Future*-style almanac full of statistics from the season and once players had all been auctioned you then learnt your fact 'week by week'. Despite all these obvious flaws, it still stands head and shoulders above the awful franchised versions of Monopoly that get trotted out every year. When will people learn that whether it's got *Game of Thrones* characters or Disney films on it, it's still the same bloody game! It's awful and boring and after three hours of no progress and even less fun, the only money you care about is the 30 quid you spent on it and the only jail on your mind is the one where you will live once you murder your family for making you play it. Awful and boring. Where Fantasy Manager differs from other 90s board game aberrations like The Neighbours Game (also real) is that somehow, 25 years on, it has become a whole lot more playable. No one remembers the finer details of a football season from a quarter of a century ago and so we tracked down a copy of the game, bought it and played it for old time's sake. Well that, and because Monopoly is awful and boring. First things first: you will definitely find this game funny when you play it with your friends. It feels like a real-life version of the talking heads shows on digital TV like *I Remember Football in 1994,* except you don't have Nasty Nick from *Big Brother* or Gina Yashere telling you why something is funny. You'll also catch yourself forever finding it humorous to buy the likes of Gary Mabbut or Ian Dowie for £0.3m, and it doesn't take long before every fourth player you auction segways into some reminiscing and YouTube hunting to relive the glory days or settle an argument about a goal they scored or a hairstyle they may or may not have had. It's not just a board game, it's a time capsule – an excuse to relive an entire season you thought you'd forgotten about. A slight warning is that it makes you feel incredibly old. Everything from the match reports to the transfer fees makes you realise your own mortality that tiny bit more. Not to mention that many of the players you can buy have sadly passed away. Nothing like a deceased midfield four to really suck the fun out of a game. You are also reminded now and then that it is a board game and you do have to eventually finish it. It has all the 'chance' cards trappings that come with a board game, where you might get an injury or a televised game generates £1.5m from the bank, but the truth is you just want to read old scores with your mates and remember how great Robbie Fowler was.

Bridging the gap between children learning how to auction via board games, premium phone lines and the game we now know was a whole lot of rival newspapers and websites offering very similar versions of the game. With the noughties bringing in next-generation consoles and overseeing the death of traditional games like Subbuteo, Fussball and Slap the Butcher, fantasy football became a free-for-all for anyone with a website as they all aimed to monopolise a captive audience. Talking of Monopoly, wasn't it awful and boring?! Papers started offering a million quid to the overall winner and yet I still insisted on picking Neil Ruddock. It wasn't until around 2012 that the Premier League's own version of the game really became synonymous with fantasy football as a whole. The truth as to why that happened is likely because no one ever cared about the million quid on offer. The prize might as well have been a trip to Oz with a unicorn and Rihanna, it was that fictional to us. It wasn't like you cared who won at the end. You paid attention until your own interest had waned, like the Olympics when the British athletes go out. The Premier League version mastered the mini-league element, where for the first time you got an opportunity to learn how to really hate your friends and play the game at the same time. That is still truly the essence of any season of fantasy football, even with the modern draft or daily versions on offer. They also pioneered the now standard format of picking a captain for double points and a wildcard that allows unlimited transfers for a specific period of time. There's been some shit along the way, sure (All Out Attack chip anyone?), but the fact that it had all the pretty kit pictures that were fully licensed and it was free to play, not a penis pump phone number in sight, meant that it was and is the go-to website if you want to get a disciplinary at work. Fantasy football really has come a long way from broadsheet papers and premium phone lines to an easily accessible online phenomena played by millions and millions of people across the globe. Some of us have grown with the sport and been there in the early days to watch its evolution into the behemoth it has slowly become. Some have only known the game in its more recent incarnations and would never be able to fathom that there was a time when it wasn't played online – to be honest, those same people probably can't fathom that there was ever a time without the internet at all. And while, yes, we probably all want to punch those individuals in the face for being too young to know about VHS, Snake on the Nokia and Teletext, it's testament to the success of fantasy football that they, like us, can't imagine a world without it now. A world without the heartache, the elation, the regret, the mind games, the weeks of planning and the last-minute acts that ruin it all. Truly beautiful stuff. Long may it continue; here's to The Albini Babies.

Life is What Happens When You're Busy Playing Fantasy Football

'Time is what we want most, but what we use worst.' – William Penn

'I'm not a breakfast eater.' – Sean Penn

EVEN if you're not someone who takes fantasy football overly seriously, there will be many people who think the time you *do* spend on it is too much. Those people are, of course, people who don't play fantasy football at all. They probably assume that a hobby or pastime like that should take up no more time than, say, watching *Eastenders* a couple of times a week if it happens to be on when you're flicking through the channels. Personally, I haven't watched *Eastenders* since Phil Mitchell was addicted to crack cocaine … for two weeks. That doesn't really show the severity of crack addiction, does it? Two weeks, then it was never mentioned again. We're led to believe that Phil just shrugged it off, are we? Maybe went for a brisk walk? Had a bit of Calpol, felt better and saw sense? Not to mention the fact that *Eastenders* couldn't actually portray Phil taking that most terrible of drugs on a pre-watershed broadcast, so all they could do to signify that Phil Mitchell, this once mighty, respected man, had succumbed to this crippling addiction was to put a little black woolly hat on his head. That was it. A tiny black, woolly hat was the full extent of it. Sure, he had a bit of makeup on to make him look a little more tired than usual, and most of his scenes were done whilst sat on the floor, but essentially Phil Mitchell's entire foray into the nightmare of class-A drugs consisted of sitting down with a hat on for a fortnight.

I just worry that any impressionable youngsters that might have been watching the whole inaccurate sorry state of affairs unfold could have easily been under the impression that a full-blown crack cocaine addiction isn't something to overly worry about. Sure, you'll have some questionable taste in headwear for a bit, but after that you'll be right as rain, as if nothing happened at all. If you would like to hear any of our other opinions on plotlines from *Eastenders* across the years, please feel free to buy our upcoming spin-off book *The Albert Squares Present: The A-Z of Walford*.

Fantasy football is enjoyed at various levels of seriousness, and some people have more time than others. If a brain surgeon was spending 40 hours a week on spreadsheets and graphs for his six different fantasy football teams, then that's probably a bit excessive and you might not want to be under his knife, especially the Monday after his Triple Captain gamble didn't work out. But for someone who sits behind a desk for 40 hours a week in a job they either don't care about or don't fully understand, then an addiction to fantasy football is almost mandatory. If that's you, then you have time. A lot of it.

Maybe you have the time to research every player's recent stats, seeing as you're bored at work. Maybe you have the time to look into how each player has played in previous seasons against their upcoming game-week opponent in more depth, seeing as you're bored at work. Maybe you have time to predict each player's likely scores over the next month using a simple algorithm, seeing as you're bored at work. Maybe you tell your other half that you're working late so that you can take that information and put it into a colour-coded spreadsheet and accompanying Venn diagram, seeing as you're bored at work.

As long as the time and effort you are putting into fantasy football isn't affecting your life and your loved ones, then carry on. If, however, you've put *so much* time and effort into fantasy football that you *don't have* a life or any loved ones as a direct result, then you might as well carry on too. The scale of fantasy football seriousness is wide, from a mere #1: 'I'll create a team at the start of the season with every intention of giving it a go this year, but I'll ultimately forget my password and never look at it, or think about it again', to a #10: 'I've been cautioned by the police for attempting to contact the next-door neighbour of the third-choice Leicester right-back to see if he's likely to be playing midweek'.

There will always be something better you can be doing other than looking, tinkering, planning or researching your fantasy football team. Surely something needs paying, organising, cleaning or feeding. Ultimately, there's probably something else in your life that needs that sort of attention to detail. But fantasy football is the ultimate procrastination from life. It feels as if what you are doing is important even if it isn't. Not to mention that in any office-based job, a fantasy football-related spreadsheet looks an awful lot like a non-fantasy football related spreadsheet from, well, pretty much any distance at all, so it can be very easy to get away with.

The fantasy football spreadsheet is often the thing of ridicule. Is it rather excessive to create a database of fixtures or form, or fixtures *and* form? Yes. Yes, it probably is. But ultimately, you'll be reaping the rewards from having the information in front of you and colour coded for easy use. Plus, it will more than likely be your mates that play fantasy football but don't have a spreadsheet who are the ones taking the piss. Granted, if you're being mocked for creating a spreadsheet by the cool guy at work – let's call him Chad – who doesn't play fantasy football because he's too busy either making love to lingerie models, washing his 50-grand sports car or winning bodybuilding competitions, then yeah, maybe you should feel ashamed. But if the scorn is being poured on you by a fantasy footy-playing pal who goes on websites to look at spreadsheets that *someone else* has made, then you really don't need to worry as they don't have a leg to stand on. Personally, have I ever created a spreadsheet? No. I'm too busy doing most of the things that cool guy Chad is, although perhaps to a slightly lesser extent; maybe the ladies haven't known they've been modelling lingerie when I took those photos, and maybe I don't wash my Ford Focus as much as I should and, yes, *maybe* I missed the Wokingham regional qualifiers for Mr Universe because I was queueing up for a sausage roll in Greggs. But I'm not a spreadsheet creator, I'm an occasional spreadsheet observer. That is the difference.

While there are varying degrees of how seriously people play 'the game of the beautiful game', I believe there are just three different types of people; three categories that you will fall into as a fantasy football player:

The Casual
Fantasy Football Seriousness Level 0–3

Typical Characteristics:
Humorous, yet incredibly common team name based around a pun on a player's name, e.g. *Pique Blinders, Tikka Mo Salah, Lallanas in Pyjamas.*

When asked if they play fantasy football will usually answer with a wince, grimace or a smile of regret. 'I've tried but I'm shit' / 'I have a go but I forget to look at it after the second week'.

Keen enough on football, but will always pick players whose names they recognises from several years ago when they used to watch more football – before the kids and the mortgage. The Casual's game-week one team will consist of James Milner, Jack Wilshere and Joe Hart, and will stay that way until the end of the season.

Bonus Fact:
The Casual is only referred to as 'The Casual' by The 'Expert'. The Casual doesn't care that he is referred to as 'The Casual' and thinks The 'Expert' is a weirdo and a condescending twat.

The Player
Fantasy Football Seriousness Level 4–8

Typical Characteristics:
An equally humorous yet slightly more original and less-widely used team name, e.g. *Delph and Safety, Xhaka Khan, Ivory Toast, Can of Bayern Bru.*

When asked if they play fantasy football, will answer, simply, 'Yeah, I play'.

They're keen. Main focus is to beat their mates in the mini-league (probably called 'The League of Not So

Extraordinary Gentlemen'). Sometimes, on rare occasions, this drive can force The Player to do some extreme and desperate things. The Player won't forget a transfer deadline apart from the occasional random Friday kick-off or one of those stupid two-day long Christmas game weeks. They're happy to be a sporadic spreadsheet observer but will never get around to creating their own. Tends to get better and better each season. Pretty happy to finish in the top 150,000 every year but doesn't know what that rank means as an overall percentage and doesn't really care.

Bonus Fact:

Very much like Pokemon, The Player can evolve into The 'Expert' with just one very successful season. Negatives of this transformation include finding the game of fantasy football less fun the more brilliant you begin to find yourself. You may also start creating your own logo to use in your profile picture on social media. If you find this happening, please seek medical advice as soon as possible.

The 'Expert'
Fantasy Football Seriousness Level 9–10+

Typical Characteristics:

Non-humorous team name that can be very specific to the player, e.g. *Clive's Xi, The Fantasy Football Team of Dave Walsh, The FPL Sargeant's Squad, Six Seasons Ago I Came in the Top 0.3%.*

When asked if they play fantasy football, will answer with a snigger, 'Just a bit'.

The 'Expert' is good at fantasy football. There's no two ways about it. The time, effort, blood, sweat, tears and highlighter fluid they put into it means they've become good. Is there really a skill to fantasy football? That's a different discussion for a different time, but The 'Expert' has been doing something right, and their consistently high finish every season is a testament to that. In the greater scheme of things, is there actually anything tangible to show for it at the end of the day other than some decent-looking figures on their season history? No. But then again, if they're happy, then they've ultimately won. Except there can actually only be one winner every season, and, let's be honest, they're never actually an expert, they're usually some bloke from India who got lucky and who's half-decent at maths.

Bonus Fact:

In most circumstances, an actual 'Expert' will refer to himself as an 'Expert'. However, someone who doesn't qualify as an 'Expert', other than the fact that they too make spreadsheets and fancy themselves at fantasy football, will *also* refer to themselves as an 'Expert'. The real 'Expert' is worth listening to for tips, if you can stop him talking about his overall rank in the 2009/10 season for five minutes. The fake 'Expert', however, will sell you bullshit all day long. The problem is, it all sounds like it could be good advice.

When you're desperate to succeed at fantasy football, you'll look anywhere and everywhere for information that gives you even the slightest of advantages, for a little-known stat, fact or piece of whispered gossip that will give you the edge on the competition. Points will be the reward for the time you put in and the research you did whilst you should have been buying your parents a wedding anniversary gift. But you weren't there the day they got married; it was nine months before you were even born for Christ's sake, so if you actually think about it, it doesn't *really* matter. What *does* matter, however, is that these golden nuggets of information that you have picked up may very well elevate you through the ranks in your mini-league. Sweaty Keith in your mini-league doesn't know that Sergio Agüero *always* scores against Newcastle, and that @BobTheInjuryBoffin on Twitter reckons that not only is Jamie Vardy back training with the starting 11 again, but he's looking sharper than ever. Halitosis Steven hasn't got a clue that, with an injury to their normal attacking-midfielder, Everton are almost certainly going to be playing their £4.5m second-choice right-back in that role and that there's a chance Alexis Sanchez won't get the full 90 minutes this week because of woman (dog) trouble. You just need to beware of false prophets, because wherever there is fantasy football, the fantasy football charlatan is lurking somewhere nearby and your ridiculous level of dedication to finding out the inside scoop may be in vain.

Some actors put on weight for a role. You see them in interviews – already back to being sickeningly beautiful and skinny again, by the way – claiming how hard it was sitting on their sofa and eating ice cream all day, every day for two months for a job that was going to pay them 30 million dollars. Call me cynical, but I don't think it's that hard. Pay me 30 million dollars and I'll spend every day sat down eating junk food. In fact, just give me 20 quid and I'll do it, as long as you pay for the ice cream as well. I understand that losing the weight is the difficult bit, but when you've got tens, if not *hundreds,* of millions in the bank, you can probably afford a treadmill and a personal trainer, I would have thought. Don't get me wrong, putting on six stone for an acting role is a definite commitment, but the rewards, i.e. the 30 million dollars, outweigh that commitment.

The rewards for commitment shown to fantasy football are a lot less gratifying than the previously stated obscene monetary value. But the risks are far greater. Don't believe me? Why don't you ask an American gentleman called Evan Brady. We were contacted several years ago by a listener to our show from across the pond in the US of A. He informed us that his girlfriend had just given birth to a happy, healthy baby boy. Wonderful news. Get the lad a Gaffer Tapes baby grow from our online merchandise store. Many listeners, over the years, have got in touch when they've been blessed with their very own addition to the next generation of fantasy football managers, and the subsequent pictures they send of the little one are always a treat – especially if the baby is rocking some Gaffer merch'. But Evan Brady took his commitment to fantasy football to the next level …

When my wife was in labour, I spent the entire duration attempting to stroke her hair, hold her hand and do all the things I had both seen on television and remembered from the bits of the antenatal class I actually paid attention to. My wife, however, was upside down in a hospital bed, screaming at me to stop touching her while I attempted to stop her falling on her head. But regardless of my incompetence on that fateful day, I was present, I was eager to help and I was happy to be shouted at – three disciplines I continue to employ in parenting. But when Evan Brady's other half was in labour, he had a very different agenda.

As his beloved was deep into one of the most terrifying, life-changing moments a human being will experience – bringing a life, *another being,* into this glorious world – Evan Brady left the room to set his fantasy football line-up. Yep. Let that particular feat of heroism sink in for a minute. The guy stepped out of the labour ward while his girlfriend was giving birth to their son to make sure his captain was set and his bench in order. What a bloody hero.

We'd like to add the caveat that Evan didn't actually miss the birth of his son, and if he had have then I don't think we would feel quite as comfortable joking about it. But on that fateful day, Evan committed, he prioritised – if only for a brief moment – and decided that he had to take action. Fantasy football line-ups don't just set themselves, much is the tragedy. Maybe there was a chance that he would miss the first few seconds of his son's life, maybe his wouldn't be the first face that his little boy saw when he entered this crazy race that we call life, but he had to make sure the armband was on Harry Kane and that he started Raheem Sterling over Riyad Mahrez.

As a writer, it is almost compulsory to procrastinate. You won't be able to tell, but halfway through the previous sentence, between the words 'almost' and 'compulsory', I stopped for 15 minutes to watch a compilation video of dogs getting shocks from pissing on electric fences. It's the excuse to do anything but the task you are actually supposed to be doing. Yes, I need to put all those boxes in the shed before it rains this afternoon, but I've got some unclean pennies that I need to put in a glass of Coca-Cola because I have *always* wanted to see if that actually works. I understand that I need to get the windscreen wipers on the car fixed, but I need to make doodles of what my personalised professional wrestling championship belt would look like before I forget!

The beauty of fantasy football is that it is not something you procrastinate *from*, but something you procrastinate *to*. It becomes the task you undertake when you can't be bothered to do the thing you know deep down you really should be spending that time on. The best bit is, it's more worthwhile than a useless procrastination like getting lost in a YouTube wormhole of Gordon Ramsay yelling at Americans until they cry. In fact, if you're completely honest with yourself, it's probably *more* important than the original task you're procrastinating from. Maybe there are 99 other more important things that you could be doing instead of researching, planning and tinkering with your fantasy football team, but there are probably 999 less important ones. I like those stats, and if there's one thing us fantasy football managers appreciate, it's a good stat. You can pass it off as work, as something important. You can either pretend you're doing something else, as we all do when we're sat in the office squinting in contemplation at the screen – because a fantasy football-related squint of contemplation at a screen looks very much like a work-related squint of contemplation at a screen. Go on, try it … see. On the other hand, you can hold your hands up and admit that you are, in fact, spending time on your fantasy football team when you should be doing something else, but that fantasy football is, in fact, important. Technically it *is* a game and there *are* prizes, regardless of which website you use to play your fantasy football on. There are cash sums, holidays, VIP tickets to the football, computer games and goody bags all up for grabs for being good at fantasy football. So, if you are going to be playing, why not play to win some stuff. That way any procrastination is warranted. It's validated in your own mind and to your other half/boss/tax man/parole officer or anyone else who may question why you haven't done all the other stuff that you're supposed to have done.

Is your husband or wife going to be thinking about that knackered windscreen wiper or those wet boxes in the garden when you hand them a substantial amount of cash, probably presented in the form of one of those aesthetically pleasing fans of money or a massive oversized cheque like those (definitely fake) Postcode Lottery adverts? Absolutely not, it won't matter at all. Will your boss be annoyed that you spent seven hours a day tweaking your team and looking up hundreds of stats instead of doing your actual job when you're on a luxury holiday? Yeah, almost certainly. They'll be utterly fucking furious, unless you take your boss with you, that is. If, however, you are a realist who knows that there are millions and millions of people who play fantasy football, and therefore the likelihood of you winning a prize is probably pretty slim, not to mention the fact that you're shit, then maybe, instead, you need some tips on how to avoid procrastinating and wasting time playing the game we call fantasy football.

As a stand-up comedian – something else that is prone to a monumental amount of procrastination on a day-to-day basis – I found that I talked about masturbating on stage a lot. Well, they say write about what you know. In my research into the subject, which I had been extensively committed to since the age of 13, I came across a website (not literally) that gave Christian people tips on how to avoid masturbating. It said that it was unclean and an abomination towards the Lord if they were to masturbate and that they wouldn't get into heaven as a result. The particular article sympathises and understands that it is not easy to avoid masturbating, and the tips provided are a guide on how to live a more wholesome, holy, pure life as a result of never *ever* practising onanism.

I felt I had hit the comedy jackpot when I saw the three tips written by someone so wildly out of touch with reality and how the average human works and thinks. Below are the three verbatim tips on how a good Christian should avoid masturbating, plus my expert take on why they are so utterly ridiculous.

Tips on how to avoid masturbating:

1. When you bathe, do not admire yourself in a mirror. Simply wash yourself quickly and get dressed.

Who's doing that? Who – on earth – is getting turned on looking at themselves in a mirror? What kind of narcissistic pervert can't keep their hands off themselves after catching a glimpse of their naked reflection? 'Jesus Christ, I look good in the bath. Come here, you!' And who can see themselves in a mirror while they're in the bath? I am in my 30s and I have partaken in many a bath over the course of my life, my friend, but I can safely say that I have never been in a bath and been able to see myself in a mirror at the same time.

2. Never touch the intimate parts of your body except during normal toilet processes. Avoid being alone as much as possible. Find good company and stay in this good company.

First of all, who uses the phrase 'toilet processes'? I think this very clinical use of language is probably used to take any sexual connotation out of said toilet process. But let's be completely honest, does anyone feel sexy on the toilet? If you do, then you probably have bigger problems than masturbating, and you should definitely stay away from

B&Q show bathrooms. Avoiding being alone as much as possible is probably a sure-fire way of stopping yourself masturbating, as, unless you're Louis C.K., you're unlikely to do it in front of people at a social event. But the whole 'find good company and stay in this good company' part feels a tad desperate, doesn't it? I can just imagine a sexually frustrated Christian fella begging his mates not to leave him alone at 2am: 'Don't go! Please, just one more game of Boggle! JUST ONE MORE GAME OF BOGGLE!'

3. If the temptation seems overpowering while you are in bed, get out of bed and go into the kitchen and fix yourself a snack, even if it is in the middle of the night, and even if you are not hungry.

Right. If over the course of my life I had to get up and eat a cheese sandwich every time I was lying in bed thinking about masturbating, I would be 28 fucking stone. I'd be going to heaven alright, but at the age of 40 from a massive heart attack.

The whole point of this seemingly pointless digression isn't just to highlight the ridiculousness of the frigid Christian geezer who wrote the article which got me rebooked in many a comedy club across the south-east of England over the years. It has also inspired me to create my own tips on how to avoid the temptations of fantasy football when you really should be doing something else. I hope, my children, that you take heed of the three simple suggestions below, in the hope that they lead you to live a much more wholesome and, more importantly, *productive* life.

Tips on how to avoid Fantasy Footballing:

1. Do not, under any circumstances, find yourself alone with a computer or laptop late at night after just having watched *Match of the Day*. Your mind will be full of desiring thoughts brought on directly by having just watched so much action. You'll have different scenarios and different men running around your thoughts, but please try to focus. Go straight to bed. Maybe don't even brush your teeth.

2. Refrain from sitting behind your desk at work during any period of inactivity. If you find yourself becoming bored, why not ask your boss for some more work to do. The act of hard work and focus will help stop your hands wandering to your mouse. Think pure, wholesome, productive thoughts.

3. Make a list. Write down all the things you are going to spend time doing instead of fantasy football. Not all tasks have to be boring; why not start a stamp collection or begin constructing a fleet of Airfix model airplanes? Walk a dog. Don't have a dog – ask to walk a neighbour's. Neighbour doesn't have a dog – walk the neighbour. An eventful, active life with great companionship will help you combat the urge to fantasy football. Soon, your previous mucky fantasies will be a distant memory.

So, whether you are a casual who forgets his login details before the end of August or an 'expert' who lives, breathes and oozes fantasy football, you will probably have been able to identify with some aspects. You will have likely recognised the amount of time and level of commitment *you* give to fantasy football. There is no right and wrong answer here. As long as you're happy and not hurting anyone, yourself included (I once knew someone who injured their hand punching Dele Alli's fantasy Premier League profile picture on their computer screen), then good luck to you. Spend five minutes a week playing fantasy football, spend five hours a day, who cares? Crack on, my friend. But for Christ's sake, put those boxes in the shed and get that fucking windscreen wiper fixed first, it's started raining!

'Time you enjoy wasting is not wasted time.' –

Marthe Troly-Curtin

'With short hair, you have to get a haircut every two or three weeks. And if you're colouring your hair, you have to colour it that often.' –

Jamie Lee Curtis

What Are They On About?

WITH a pastime as involved, as meta and, yes, as *geeky* as fantasy football, you'll need to know the lingo. Don't get us wrong, this isn't cockney rhyming slang, prison terminology or the kind of covert codewords and phrases used by the Mafia when there's a chance the FBI are listening into their conversations. This is far, far more serious ... and cringey. So, don't feel left out of the loop when the fantasy football boffins and spreadsheet warriors are discussing how they're getting on a fixture-proof bandwagon for the DGW to help their OR, with our handy guide to fantasy football terminology.

1. Differential

Pete: 'You captaining Lukaku this week?'

Fred: 'No, I'm going with Mitrović, his percentage-picked is a lot less and I think he'll score. He's a great differential.'

Differential isn't a dirty word. *Sphincter* is a dirty word. *Nosh* is a positively filthy word. But despite the disdain associated with it on our podcast, *differential* isn't. A differential pick is essentially a player with a low percentage ownership, an unlikely pick if you will. By choosing to include this fella in your team, you're not playing safe, not going with the majority, some may say you're a rebel – someone who doesn't conform to social norms, like a young Nick Knowles. If your differential pick works, you'll not only look like the coolest kid at school, sat on your chair the wrong way around at the back of the class, but you'll also be showered in points. Hot, thick, glorious points. All the sheep are picking Kane, Agüero and/or Aubameyang – you're selecting Danny Ings. The squares are clamouring for Pogba, Dele Alli and Mané – you're breezing in, cool as a bloody cucumber, with a cheeky little bit of Andros Townsend. Those robots are awarding the captain's armband to Salah, Sterling or KDB – you've stuck it on Aaron motherfucking Lennon. Of course, the odds are not in your favour if you pick a differential, it's likely that the majority are right; that's why that player is picked by the majority, because he's quite simply a bit better and more likely to get fantasy football points. But sometimes, just sometimes, it works. As many that play fantasy football do, I have my own differential anecdote. Well, 'anecdote' is probably a bit strong, I just captained Salomón Rondón when he got a hat-trick of headers against Swansea in 2016. That's the extent of it. It's unlikely to win any awards for storytelling and I doubt I'll be looking to publish it as an audiobook (unless our publishers are reading this and thinking it's definitely got legs), but let's be honest it's pretty impressive, right? I brought him in, he did the business and then I took him back out again. He was covert, effective and mysterious, disappearing again into the night, his mission fulfilled, like Zorro or the Milk Tray Man, if Zorro or the Milk Tray Man could only play 70 minutes and had no left foot whatsoever. I looked pretty knowledgeable, and more importantly cool, rolling off on my skateboard into the sunset with all my lovely, beautiful Rondón points, with my baseball cap on backwards, chewing gum. The hundreds of times that I've tried it and it has failed don't matter, it's the *one* time it succeeds that you'll remember, well, that you'll tell people about at least, hopefully in the form of a lucrative audiobook.

2. Bandwagon

Pete: 'Are you bringing in that Watford centre-back who scored last week?'

Fred: 'Why do you keep asking me what I'm doing? Live your own life, Pete. No, he won't do it again this week, that's a bandwagon I'm not jumping on.'

One-hit wonders in music are a commonly discussed topic over a few beers in the pub. Everyone will have a different nominee and reasons why it is the best, but ultimately there really is no correct answer to what the greatest one-hit wonder of all time is, apart from the fact that it is definitely 'Would I Lie to You?' by Charles and Eddie, and that's the end of the discussion. It just so happens that football often throws up its own one-hit wonders, too. Every now and then a player will do something great, just the once, and everyone is all over them doing the Macarena and letting off 99 red balloons in celebration. Karel Poborský springs to mind. The Czech winger and lesbian hobbit lookalike scored one very good goal at Euro '96 and got signed by Manchester United, arguably the biggest club in the world at the time. Poborský's time at United is generally referred to as a flop, where he amassed just over 30 appearances and only six goals in 18 months. While Poborský isn't the worst impulsive signing made off the back of just one decent moment, it is still very much the definition of a bandwagon.

In fantasy football, bandwagons are formed, jumped on and leapt off very quickly. One player you had never heard of before does something good, a handful of people buy him in the hope it's the start of something long term, more and more people see this happen and they want part of the action too before his price goes up, and, BANG, that's how you get yourself a bandwagon. A perfect example of a bandwagon is just after Tottenham defender Juan Foyth, owned by a grand total of 84 Fantasy Premier League managers (out of nearly six million), scored the only goal in Tottenham's November 2018 win over Crystal Palace. Foyth got points for the goal, the clean sheet and all three bonus points, bringing in a total haul of 15 – pretty good for an afternoon's work. Over 30,000 people decided to jump on that bandwagon and transfer Foyth into their side, and do you know what he did the next week? Nothing, well technically he got two points. And the week after that? Nothing, *actually* nothing as he scored a big fat zero when Spurs conceded four against their North London rivals Arsenal. He subsequently went on to play a mere 90 minutes in his next seven matches. Bandwagon status: squashed into a tiny cube at the scrap yard, recycled and currently being used as reinforcing supports on Alan Brazil's studio swivel chair.

Some bandwagons work, and it pays off to get on board early. When Liverpool's Andrew Robertson's bandwagon took off in 2017, not only was the young lad playing fantastically at the very top level, but he was pulling in huge fantasy football points to boot, with an abundance of assists and clean sheets. Some said it was a fad, that he was going to be a flash in the pan, but that bandwagon kept on rolling. In fact, as I sit and write this, that particular bandwagon has ceased to stop. Sure, it's slowed down on the odd occasion, but that's just natural. Andrew Robertson has gone from a differential to one of the very first names on any fantasy football team sheet. In fact, the bandwagon doesn't exist anymore, he's transcended beyond the wagon to something else. Maybe a chariot? Yes, a golden chariot led by unicorns that the majority of us travel on the back of every weekend.

My problem is that I will watch a bandwagon begin to move off slowly and I assume that the knee jerkers are wrong to be hopping on board so early. So I wait. A couple of game weeks go by and the player is still performing, his price is rising and the bandwagon is moving pretty damn quick. I keep my nerve and remain stationary. Then, the next thing I know, the player is an absolute essential, everyone else is riding the shit out of that goddamn thing and I am forced to pay an absolutely extortionate price to get involved as well, or I'll be falling too far behind everyone else. I should have jumped.

As a result, and with this in mind, I find myself occasionally anticipating a bandwagon, hoping it's a Robertson and not a Foyth; a Charles and Eddie and not a Baha Men. But inevitably, as is the way with the fantasy football gods, my risk doesn't work out, that rickety old pile of crap breaks down before it can even get moving, the sound of 'Who Let the Dogs Out?' on the busted cassette player.

3. Fixture proof

Pete: 'Jamie Vardy is away to Chelsea this week; if I had him in my team, I think I'd drop him to the bench.'

Fred: 'Is this your way of asking me what I'm doing without actually asking me, Pete? You're so weird! No, I wouldn't drop Vardy just because he's away to Chelsea. He's scored against everyone this season; he's pretty fixture proof.'

Depending what fixture calendar you use, or what spreadsheet you tend to look at when planning your next few game weeks, the nicer fixtures, the Crystal Palace at home type fixtures, tend to be as green as the freshly cut summer grass, or as blue as the unadulterated, cloudless sky above it. However, the colour of a bad fixture, a

Manchester City away, is a dark red, a scarlet, almost purple bloodbath of a fixture, regardless of where you look. It's the universal colour of a fucking shit time. If you're contemplating starting your West Ham centre-back on that particular crimson tide of a fixture, then you're crazy. If, however, you're thinking of not only starting a Harry Kane or perhaps an Eden Hazard, but *captaining* them, then you're clearly someone who believes in certain players being 'fixture proof' – the kind of player who will perform regardless of the opposition. It doesn't matter to them if they're playing Liverpool away or Huddersfield at home, they're colour blind when it comes to the fixture. There's a lot of truth in the old adage that big players turn up for big games – did the likes of Shearer, Henry, Rooney and Suárez not score some truly memorable worldies against the Premier League's finest as well as the lower echelons? Exactly. That, my friend, is the definition of fixture proof. In fact, if the phrase was in the dictionary, then it would probably feature a photograph of Wayne Rooney, mid-air, poised, about to connect with Nani's cross and convert that famous bicycle kick against Manchester City. Incidentally, you'd probably also have a picture of Rooney underneath the definitions of Rug, Scally and Help the Aged.

4. Double game week (DGW)

Pete: 'I've just seen that Tottenham are playing twice this week! I don't understand. I'm scared, I feel alone and I no longer know what my name is or where I live.'

Fred: 'Well, put your clothes back on and listen, Pete. It's very simple: several teams are playing twice within this game week because they missed fixtures due to having cup games a while ago; it's called a double game week.'

They might be the most talked about two words in the fantasy football calendar. They're feared, revered, meticulously planned for, overwhelming and too huge to handle without a little help. It's very similar to a Christmas turkey, or having a fat baby.

A double game week is formed when, in the mid-to-latter stages of the season, several teams have cup games that encroach upon their Premier League fixtures. This results in that team missing out on a fixture in a particular game week but being handed a second fixture in another. Typically, these double fixtures appear somewhere around game weeks 33, 34, 35 or even later. The double game week will therefore mean, of course, that there will be players who will be playing twice within a game week.

If you play the official Fantasy Premier League game, the triple captain's armband is a much talked about commodity for this double game week. Sergio Agüero or Harry Kane on a double tends to be the norm. However, I am a personal advocate of not necessarily using your triple captain chip on a double game week. Yes, the odds of a big haul are obviously more in your favour if your player is playing twice, but it's obviously not a certainty on those fixtures. For example, Agüero may be on a double game week involving an away match against a scrappy Burnley side as well as hosting Liverpool. Now, is he likely to get more points in those 180 minutes of football (assuming he even plays two full matches within a week, knowing the sort of rotation that goes on at City – please see '7. Rotation') or would it be better to hedge your bets on another game week when an in-form Agüero is at home to the bottom of the league who have the most goals conceded in the division? Let us not forget that the Argentinian's five goals against Newcastle came in a single game, well, in *twenty minutes* to be more accurate.

Whether you like playing the odds or not, the double game week most certainly does need to be planned for. There's potential to have 22 games worth of points rather than the usual 11. If you spot a DGW coming from far enough away, you can prep for it. Maybe, if you're a Fantasy Premier League player, you bench boost and get 30 games worth of points that week. There's no way that a haul like that won't affect your overall rank and bump you up in a good few of your mini-leagues. Don't fear the double game week, friends, embrace it. Make the most out of it. Use it to your advantage. Like that Christmas turkey/fat baby, make that bastard work for *you*!

5. Overall rank (OR)

Pete: 'I'm third in my mini-league!'
Fred: 'Yeah, but what's your overall rank?'
Pete: 'That's difficult. Let's see – two a day since I was 13, maybe three on weekends.'
Fred: 'What?! I'm talking about your overall rank – where you're placed out of everyone playing fantasy football.'

Pete: 'Oh … I thought you were talking about something else, Fred.'

I'm going to start by saying that technically your overall rank doesn't mean anything until the very last of the final whistles is blown of game week 38. It's nice to be able to point out a particularly good OR if and when it occurs during the season, but it's how you finish that matters. I learned that from Ron Jeremy. In April 2011 the American Samoa national football team lost 31-0 to Australia, but at one point in the game they were drawing. Does that mean American Samoa can boast about it? No. No, it doesn't. Every year, after the first game week of the season, some crazy bastard who did something ridiculous like triple captaining Watford right-back Kiko Femenía has the honour of calling themselves the number-one ranked fantasy footballer in the world. It does only last for seven days, of course, and their final overall rank will no doubt be down in the five millions as they hadn't been able to change their team due to the straightjacket. But for one day they sat atop the fantasy football mountain, and that is something that most of us will never, ever be able to boast.

Many of the undesirables on social media like to convert their overall rank into a percentage. Their rank of 55,000th in the world looks a lot better when it's referred to as 'Top 1 per cent'. The good thing about that kind of mathematics is that you can be pretty damn average at fantasy football and still appear like a genius in your Twitter bio. 'Top 14 per cent' sounds good, '770,000th' not so much.

6. Dream team

Pete: 'Aubameyang, Kane and Wilson were the top-scoring strikers this week, Fred.'

Fred: 'Yeah, that's right, they all made it into the game week 15 dream team.'

Pete: 'I had a dream about you last night, Fred.'
Fred: 'Not now, Pete.'

The dream team is that week's ultimate team, the best possible team you could have picked. It's essentially showing you what you could have won. Well screw you Jim Bowen, because I have no use for a speedboat anyway, I live in Slough! It's very rare that the team will actually belong to someone, it's usually just a collection of the best performing keeper, four defenders and midfielders and two strikers of the week. Some players tend to be in there every week, like the boffins at school you never liked – the straight-A creepy kid who gave the teacher an apple and called them by their first name at lunchtime. 'Great result in the rugby wasn't it, Gary?' It's not *Gary*, it's Mr Hales, alright? And who cares about rugby? Does anyone actually know what a good result in rugby even is? No one actually understands it, not even the people playing.

Once the season is over and all 380 Premier League games are done and dusted, there will be a dream team of the season consisting of the 11 highest-point-scoring players between the positions. The annoying thing is that in nearly all circumstances you could have afforded those 11 players if you'd have picked them at the start of the season. Before everyone jumped on them and their prices rose, there's a high possibility that you would have had the money to get those boys in, plus a semi-decent bench, perhaps filled with unlikely high point scorers from newly promoted sides. It's a hard thing to look at, but there will be some consolation in the fact that no one had that team at the start of the season and no one had it at the end. Plus, if you started that exact team in game week one the following season, despite the fact that all their prices would now be too high and you would never be able to afford them, they won't be the dream team by the end of the season. Along will come a new batch of players who have decided they would quite like to play really well this year, plus a few new names you hadn't heard of before. Of course, the likes of Harry Kane and Mo Salah will tend to be in there again, but who's going to be the *next* Salah? The guy who everyone kind of remembers from when he was at Chelsea, but doesn't really consider as an option, who then goes on to have such an incredible debut season in the Premier League that he is featured in the dream team nearly every single week and holds the record for the most fantasy football points in a single season. What a player. Bet he's got a speedboat.

7. Rotation

Pete: 'I don't understand why Sterling didn't play, he scored a hat-trick the week before!'

Fred: 'He's just been rotated for Gabriel Jesus this week, that's all. He'll probably play next week.'

Pete: 'You know everything, don't you Pete? Did you know I had a dream about you last night?'

Trying to work out what is going on in a manager's mind is impossible. Some managers wear their hearts on their sleeves, like Jürgen Klopp; however, some, like Pep Guardiola, are harder to read than an abstract poem by an illiterate tribesman from the remotest jungle in Papua New Guinea, that's been carved into a frog, using another frog. Guardiola is notorious for rotating the Manchester City starting line-up. Not a big problem, I hear you say (well, I don't hear *you* say, as I am assuming from the fact that you're reading a book about fantasy football that you know why it's a problem. I'm actually talking to that person behind you, the one with a life, who *doesn't* read books about fantasy football). That Manchester City squad is full of so much quality that Pep has the luxury of being able to rotate players. That person behind you probably also thinks it's really nice to see so many of the boys get a regular run around. God, I hate that person behind you.

There's nothing more frustrating than transferring in a player, especially if he's expensive, only to have him not even be named in the squad for the very next game. It's the inexplicable randomness of the rotation that will kill you. For no reason, your new acquisition doesn't get a single minute of game time and the young academy lad who plays in his position gets the nod over him. What?! Give us a chance over here! Then the next week, if you've held your nerve and not transferred him back out again in frustration, he'll likely score some great points. Maybe he plays again the following week, all's right with the world again, the sun is shining, the birds are … BANG! – he gets dropped for that new Brazilian 'superstar' who hasn't played a single minute all season. Maybe he goes on to play only half a game the week after that, rotated with the academy lad again the following week, then perhaps gets a couple of 90 minutes again – both of which produce two goals and an assist – before playing a mere six minutes the week after that, amassing a single point! I mean, it's a bloody minefield. That's why, unless you can read that manager, or believe you've worked out the method behind his rotation madness, you are much better off putting your vote of confidence in a player that is …

8. Nailed-on

Pete: 'Will Arnautovic play tonight?'

Fred: 'Of course he'll play, he's nailed-on.'

Pete: 'That's a bit weird, a hammer that's nailed-on! Am I right?! Yeah? You get it? Hammer? Nailed? Fred, come back!'

Yes. You need to find a player who is 'nailed-on'. Forget the rotation risks – the fellas who are either not trusted to start more than a couple of games in a row or are deemed just too valuable to play in every single game, especially the seemingly easier fixtures. No, you need that player who is a dead cert, a mainstay, a real feature in his respective team. If this lynchpin is a fantasy football point scorer, then he is going to be a much safer bet than anyone open to rotation.

Maybe the rotation risk will get more points some weeks, but it'll be the weeks where he's watching from the stands and your nailed-on player is pulling in points that you'll be glad of the certainty. It doesn't matter what the reason is for him being nailed-on, whether it's because he is the only one at his club who plays in his position, or the fact that nearly every time he plays he scores and will always get a game because of that, or if it's because the team has been struggling and as a result they can't afford not to play him for the whole game as he's one of their star men. Don't get me wrong, there are a lot of players who will play the full 90 minutes unless they pick up an injury, but it's the nailed-on players who are scoring fantasy football points regularly that you want. Then, of course, that nailed-on player becomes nailed-on in *your* team.

9. Fixture ticker

Pete: 'I brought in Charlie Daniels because he's got an easy fixture on Saturday.'

Fred: 'Yeah, but what's he doing after that?'

Pete: 'Probably having some dinner or something?'

Fred: 'No, I mean, what are his fixtures like after Saturday? You should have used a fixture ticker or spreadsheet to check.'

Planning ahead isn't always easy, and, as a result, sometimes mistakes can happen if you don't take precautions. Well, that's what my parents write in my birthday card every year. It's easy to be short-sighted in fantasy football. You know that Gylfi Sigurðsson has an amazing opportunity to get solid points next week as he's both in form and at home to the bottom of the league, but what about the following week? What about the week after that? What about the rest of the month? How are his fixtures looking from now until Christmas? A fixture ticker or similar spreadsheet can tell you.

The handy little graph helps you to assess the difficulty of fixtures for all teams, and that difficulty has a corresponding colour, so you can tell how good or bad a team's upcoming run is from a single glance. Fantasy football managers are busy people and if we can save valuable time by simply glancing at a colour-coded chart to quickly see how easy a player's upcoming fixtures are, then it gives us more time to do important things like creating colour-coded charts to quickly see how easy a player's upcoming fixtures are. As mentioned before, easier match-ups largely tend to be blue or green and the harder encounters red or purple. If you're contemplating Sigurðsson, take a quick look at his run on a fixture ticker first. If, after they host the bottom of the league, it continues to be a succession of easy and winnable games, transfer him in. If, however, it is followed by back-to-back trips to the Etihad and Stamford Bridge then a fortnight later a trudge down the road to Anfield, then maybe give Gylfi the swerve. Sometimes you'll notice a glorious run of upcoming fixtures for a team that's been in bad form. Maybe it's only four of five games, but why not pre-empt that they're going to turn things around and that some of their players are worth getting in your team. Look ahead a bit, plan in advance.

10. Coverage

When a team rises to prominence in the Premier League, like Manchester City have over the last couple of years, or the likes of Chelsea or Manchester United in past seasons, it is wise to get yourself 'coverage' in your fantasy football team. When a side is as dominant as City, or they go through a strong spell for weeks on end like Liverpool, Arsenal or Leicester have, it is imperative to get representatives from those teams into yours. This means you are, quite literally, *covered*. City win 6-0 and you have a City midfielder in your team; the chances are that he's picking up a goal or an assist. If you've got a defender, he's getting a clean sheet. All you're doing is covering bases. It's the clever thing to do when a team is either in good form, has a run of easy fixtures or are just annoyingly good like the aforementioned City.

I wasn't playing fantasy football in 2003/04, I was far too busy drinking at bus stops with fellow minors (underage people, not people working in coal mines), but if I had I would have made damn sure I had Arsenal coverage. There would have been some combination of 'Invincibles' Thierry Henry, Dennis Bergkamp, Robert Pires, Patrick Vieira and Ashley Cole. Doing anything else is just stubborn, short-sighted and will have you scrabbling around in the dark searching for points that just aren't going to come, like miners (people working in coal mines not underage people).

Pete: 'I got rid of Mané last week, I don't have any Liverpool players now.'

Fred: 'You don't have any Liverpool coverage anymore?! That's silly, they're the top-performing team over the last six weeks, you absolutely have to have a couple of Liverpool players in your team.'

Pete: 'I love you, Fred.'

Fred: 'I know. I love you too, Pete. Let's have a cuddle.'

How to Beat
Your Friends at
Fantasy Football

I F we know fantasy football fans, and we think we do, then there's a pretty good chance you're reading this chapter first. After all, that's the point of all this, isn't it? You don't go through 38 weeks of weird transfer cravings and Saturday morning sickness because it's fun. God no! You do it to be better than your friends and mercilessly remind them of this for the other 14 weeks of the year. While we can't guarantee a mini-league win, there's definitely some tips and tricks and outright cheating that we can pass on to make sure you give yourself a head start every August. Unless, of course, they also own this book and then you will all be doing exactly the same things. Your temptation will now be to tell no one about this book but please resist that temptation. Come on. Don't be a dick.

The first lesson to learn in navigating the weird world of fantasy football is to avoid know-it-alls. There's always someone who thinks they know best. Of course, we are aware of the hypocrisy of this, but *we're* alright! We've got a bloody book out! Anything unsolicited is annoying; someone giving me an unsolicited nickname that I haven't sanctioned, unsolicited conversation in the office kitchen while I'm quietly trying to make a cup of coffee and deal with my hangover, and the worst of all, unsolicited advice. Some advice is welcome: don't eat yellow snow, don't drink orange juice directly after brushing your teeth, don't drink orange snow. Advice that is thrust upon you without your prior consent, however, is not as welcome. This kind of advice often comes from an 'expert'.

The fantasy football expert is an intriguing beast. They are often clinging on to and constantly referencing their one good season, which occurred several years ago. To proudly proclaim 'top 15 percent in the 2015/16 season' on your social media is as embarrassing as it is meaningless. I finished top 30 per cent in my school cross country. I finished 60th out of about 200. About 30 kids were fat in a way that only kids in the 90s were fat, a good 40 of them just walked out of lazy rebellion and 15 to 20 of the cool kids just stopped halfway through to smoke weed. You get the picture. It's not that impressive, is it? Don't get me wrong, there is some decent fantasy football advice out there. Someone can look at recent form and realise that West Ham have conceded away from home every game so far this season and that this week they're up against a

Mesut Özil, who has the best record of home assists in the league, with an average of 0.93 per game. Pointing out stats like that might be useful and make you look like some kind of dream team rain man, but, let's be honest, you're just a virgin with a homemade database. The people you know who watch football – and I mean *really* watch football – will know more than your average stat pedlar. Only a Palace fan actually knows how Palace play and who plays well on what occasion. The rest of us catch them on the odd live game or on *Match of the Day,* but that's just not the same. So, it stands to reason that these self-titled fantasy geniuses probably don't know much more than you or your mates. Therein lies the problem. It's your mates you're trying to beat, especially the one who was fat in the 90s.

If you are thinking that somewhere there is an oracle, an enigma with an almost mystical level of fantasy football insight, then sadly you are incorrect. The self-proclaimed experts have just looked up and processed a list of data that is far too boring for the majority of us to be interested in. That's all. Although, if you really do want those stats and figures, then the weird fella on Reddit – who you would run away screaming from if you saw him ambling towards you in Tesco – is definitely the go-to goblin. Don't get me wrong, it can be hugely useful and part of us thanks them for the effort that they have gone to, putting together their advice and tips, often going as far as not washing or having interaction with anyone of the opposite sex for months on end. But beware – just because they refer to themselves as an 'expert' or, worse still, 'aficionado' in their Twitter bio doesn't make it gospel. I mean, Lenny Henry probably claims to be a 'comedian' in his.

Advice doesn't need to come from a place of ego. It can be as simple as: 'If I was you, I'd stick Giroud in this week, I think he's going to play on Saturday after his midweek form in the cup, and if he does I fancy him to score against that Southampton defence; he loves a goal from a corner and they're terrible on set pieces.' See, no ego, said in an incredibly affable, relaxed and breezy manner, probably by someone with something like 'views are my own (obviously, LOL)' in their Twitter bio. But the fantasy football obsessive doesn't want to hear from that guy and his very matter-of-fact advice based on pure football knowledge, garnered from actually watching games. He wants to hear from the false prophet on social media, the guy who sells – *actually sells* – bespoke point distribution tree maps to gullible idiots who are desperate to beat Sweaty Keith and Halitosis Steven in their mini-league. That is the tragedy. They don't want to listen to Affable Alan – the real football fan who has a Watford season ticket – when he's casually talking about captaincy choices for the upcoming game week, but they do want to know the thoughts of the guy with the Bart Simpson profile picture and 'FPL Guru' in all his social media bios, but who hasn't watched a whole match since the FA Cup Final in 2011.

You can, of course, benefit from understanding the finer points of how the game works and how to make the most of its features. If you can pick the perfect captain, nail the right formation and understand who is the king of bonus points, then it obviously puts you at a definite advantage over your rivals. Let's start with bonus points, which, let's be honest, is an absolute clusterfuck of logic.

When I was at university getting an utterly useless degree in history, I accidentally walked into the wrong lecture. Easy mistake to make. University campuses are huge and lecture halls all look the same. I was far too British to admit that I wasn't supposed to be there and thought the least embarrassing decision would be to stay put and live out a 120-minute version of just accepting the wrong coffee at Starbucks. I figured if I looked like I was meant to be there, no one would notice. I walked in with the false confidence Lee Cattermole must have used when he used to lead out a Premier League side and took my seat next to a stranger who gave me the kind of look reserved for convicts and Sunday league referees. Worst case scenario, I'd find out a bit about a period of history I didn't know much about and I could treat it like a documentary you stumbled across that could turn out to be amazing. It was a quantum physics lecture. I failed most school science exams, find *Holby City* 'too sciency' and had the audacity to take notes while a man with three PhDs gave me hours of his precious time. What I wrote on that piece of paper would rival anything my two-year-old niece has on my sister's fridge, and yet I still have a stronger grasp on that two-hour exploration of quantum physics than I do of the fantasy football bonus points system.

I like to think I can watch a football match with relative objectivity. I can appreciate the work Fernandinho can do and not just the headline grabbers who score hat-tricks and rack up rabona assists. So, I will often scribble down my predictions for who will get those coveted bonus points on a Saturday evening after watching the early kick-off. I will keep an eye out for the pass completion or pick up on the times a holding midfielder can spoil a counter-attack. I'll try to remember if a keeper has made an abnormal number of saves. Then I'll wonder what an abnormal number of saves even is! Then, at half-time, I'll sometimes weep at what my life has become and how I once had aspirations beyond spending my weekend counting corner kicks in my pants. The point is, you'll watch Firmino bag a brace, Eden Hazard run the entire game and David de Gea save a penalty with his ears, and Azpilicueta, who you forgot was even playing, will smugly pick up three points, swooping like a sober guy in a shit club at 2am. However, there are opportunities to play the odds. Strikers score goals, it's their job. As Mario Balotelli once said, you can't expect to be rewarded for something you're supposed to do, which is a good point, but then again he also once said, 'only Messi is better than me'. Midfielders, however, tend to pick up bonus points if they get themselves on the scoresheet. The likes of Sadio Mané or Lampard in days gone by will always find themselves averaging at least one bonus point per week over the course of the campaign. It is something worth factoring in when you look at their hefty price at the beginning of the season. The same goes for that priceless gem of a mis-classified striker masquerading as a midfielder. Jesse Lingard at United or Wilf Zaha at Palace may technically be midfield players but in a front three they are used much more for going forward than a midfielder in a traditional sense. Lingard, for instance, has been deployed in a front two for United, yet his goal is worth five points, not four, and almost guarantees him a bonus point come full time. This is, of course, just guesswork and gambling. Bonus points are just that. A bonus. You can't plan your squad around who you think might get the maximum three points. It's hard enough trying to work out if Burnley can keep a clean sheet against Everton, let alone whether Ben Mee might get a 90 per cent pass rate. And the hard truth is that by reading this, giving bonus points a second thought, and even knowing what bonus points are, you're already giving it more thought than the spod who decides who gets points just by their latest haircut or the imagined size of their penis. He's just guessing, so you might as well just guess too.

On the flip side of bonus points is those dreaded *minus* points. The arch nemesis of bonus points in what would be the most disappointing instalment of the Marvel franchise yet. No one likes that smug little hyphen that pops up before a perfectly good number. They're shit when you see them on the weather and they're shit when you see them on your bank balance. Guys, what about golf, I hear you say. Well guess what, golf is shit too. Unfortunately, however, minus points are annoyingly very much a part of fantasy football. Defenders and goalkeepers will obviously pick up a negative score for conceding goals but, contrary to popular belief, it is very rare you will suffer too much from this. Lots of people shy away from bottom-half team defenders for this very reason, but the likes of Burnley, Stoke, West Brom and Swansea have provided some of the best value fantasy defenders in recent years. You might hear your mates ridicule you for picking newly promoted defenders because they 'concede a lot of goals'. Let them think it. Wolves defenders like Doherty, Boly and Jonny were a revelation in the 2018/19 season and freed up good money for big-name strikers, so don't be put off by the 'goals against' column or the input of one of the people you're trying to beat! Where you really suffer point losses is red cards, missed penalties and own goals. The double-edged sword of seeing your captain step up from 12 yards can really determine whether it's going to be a good week or not.

So, I'd like us all to spare a thought for Jon Walters and all those who picked him back in January 2013 against Chelsea. Walters managed to bag two own goals from midfield and topped it off with a missed penalty in the dying minutes, ending the game on an impressive -5. You don't get points for courage, Jon. It's also worth thinking about those pesky bookings when selecting your side. If you're hell-bent on having a City defender, for example, then a little bit of research might get you those few extra points you need. Otamendi picked up nine bookings in 2017/18 to Kyle Walker's one, while making only two more league appearances. Sure, we all feel a little bit nerdy and dirty for now knowing that, but if it helps you beat the office irritant then it's a necessary evil.

The one question you will get asked every weekend incessantly is, 'Who've you captained?' That's not technically true, you will also get asked with increasing ferocity, 'Would you please get off that fucking laptop and do something?' But it will largely be, 'Who've you captained?' In fact, I'm astonished it's not been made an acronym yet. WYC? That works. Pass it on. It's the single most important choice any fantasy football manager can make. This isn't a case of the captaincy being awarded to the most experienced, respected or vocal player – a defensive general with a colossal presence and the ability to whip up a losing side with a rousing half-time speech and spur them on to turn things around. Equally, the captaincy shouldn't be handed out willy-nilly to the manager's son, for example, as was often the staple back in the days of Sunday league as a kid – *yeah, you might be the gaffer's firstborn, Stewart, but you don't deserve to lead the team out in the County Cup Final. You're 19 stone and you're missing three toes on your right foot.*

Not only can making the right captain choice double that player's points and have a huge impact on your overall score for that game week, but it can double your whole weekend, your mood and your short-term relationship with your other half, parents, children and friends. In the same way that making the wrong choice can, obviously, have the adverse effect. Zero doubled is still zero, my friend, and I guarantee that as lovely a time as you are having feeding the ducks on a Sunday with the love of your life and your adoring son and/or daughter, all you're going to be able to see as you gaze at the beautiful setting sun is a big, fat *nil points.*

We all know a guy who captained Jermain Defoe on the week he got sent off after half an hour and subsequently the minus two points he received was doubled to minus four. However, we've also all heard the fable of the friend of a friend who allocated the armband to Georginio Wijnaldum in 2015 when he put four goals past Norwich from midfield! The decision is a huge one, and one that is often the very last thing to be finalised, leaving millions of managers tinkering and wrestling with the decision right up until the minute before the deadline. Play it safe and go with your expensive centre-forward in the hope he keeps up his reliable form and bags another brace – even though that's exactly what everyone else will be doing – or be clever, go with a hunch, a possibility that, if you pull it off, could see you flying above your mates in the mini-league and gaining precious ground on all the sheep who captained the pricey striker? Do it – pull the trigger on Marouane Fellaini. Sure, he hasn't played a full 90 minutes all season and has done nothing but get a handful of yellow cards and fall over, but because of injuries *this week* he's likely to play; all the 'experts' on social media have said it, plus the team he's playing concede a lot away from home. Calculate the risk against the reward. If it works, you're the greatest. You have bragging rights for weeks (well, probably one week, until one of your mates does something better, or the balance of the universe is restored by you doing something stupid).

If your whim, your big hunch, your master plan doesn't work out and you're left looking like a fool when Fellaini did in fact come on for a pitiful seven minutes, fall over and get booked, then at least you can say you tried, goddamnit! Yes, maybe you should have just gone with the obvious choice and captained the centre-forward whose price-tag is 15 per cent of your entire team's value, like everyone else did, but you were brave, right?! Right?! No, you probably should have just captained Harry Kane, mate.

Because of Fellaini's calamitous cameo, there's no consolation that you had the vice-captain's armband on Kane. In fact, if anything, it makes it more annoying that Fellaini waddled on and ruined the possibility that your vice-captain choice almost, *almost,* made up for your mistake and saved the day. That's the eternal frustration of the vice-captain.

The VC is second choice, the ugly one who is sat on their own at the party, the silver medallist no one remembers – or the man who can haunt you if you pick wrong, who can save you if you pick *right* and will forever have a soft spot in your heart in years to come because of his one, valiant effort. That, and the fact that your captain didn't play a single minute. Like that girl from every awful American teen movie that you thought was an unattractive geek, but who took the glasses off, popped on a dress and walked down the stairs in slow motion to *that* song from *Sixpence None the Richer,* your vice-captain can prove to be your world, your everything, your silent hero, and they were right there in front of your eyes the whole time. God, I miss Freddie Prinze Jr.

Allocating the vice-captain's armband seems an afterthought, a pointless tradition like singing 'Auld Lang Syne' or going to church. But, occasionally, giving the decision just a little bit of consideration could make all the difference. Like removing your glasses and running a brush through your hair, if you make a bit of effort, maybe Freddie Prinze Jr will want to shag you too. Think about it.

Picture the scenario: your star forward, Mr Big Bucks up front, the expensive addition to your team that means you've had to compromise and buy that Wolves defender who is the cheapest player in the game and has never got a single minute on an actual football pitch in his career, is not playing. No! In fact, he's not only *not playing*, he's not in the squad. No and no again! The club's official Twitter account has released the line-up and you can't see his name, not even on the bench. Maybe you're dyslexic. That's it, you can't read properly, that must be the reason, he has to be there somewhere. They wouldn't just leave him out of the squad entirely, would they? But no, you haven't suddenly lost the ability to read English words in the last five minutes – he's not in the matchday squad. How did this happen? Is he injured? Is he being rested? It doesn't really matter. All that matters is where you placed that vice-captain's armband when you organised your team on Thursday morning, bleary eyed, supping an instant Kenco at your desk and wishing you hadn't been too lazy to get a proper coffee on your way into work. Where *did* you put that vice-captain's armband again? Your second most expensive striker? Your top-scoring midfielder? Oh god, maybe you left it on the defender you thought would have a good points return a fortnight ago but is currently in shakier form than a hungover Shakin' Stevens drinking a Shake Shack milkshake whilst shaking hands with the Iron Sheikh.

This is when heroes are made. This is when a footballer you had never given any more thought to, other than a quick click of the mouse, can rise like the proverbial salmon and save your game week; no, *make* your game week. Any decent points from your vice-captain are welcome, but anything over the average is a plus. He gets an assist; well, that's a welcome surprise, I shall thoroughly enjoy the fruits of his labour when the weekend is finally over and his points are doubled. He scores a goal; well, what an utter treat, my luck is in and as a result I will reward myself with a can of cold lager and a self-satisfactory grin. He scores a hat-trick; I'm noshing him off in a hotel room on SnapChat.

Do you tell anyone that this huge points haul is because of a stroke of luck? That your first choice essentially turned you down so you had to make do with his ugly mate, and you grew to love him? No. Unless your mates realise, you keep schtum, boast that it was all a completely intentional stroke of genius. Only you will know. You and Freddie Prinze Jr.

Another area of afterthought that can be the difference between you getting a steak dinner or having to buy your mates a new vacuum cleaner (we don't know what your mini-league is about, you'd be surprised) is the unsexiest of all the positions: substitutes. It's hard to believe for the modern football fan, but the concept of substitutions was only introduced to the actual game in 1965. Even then they were not introduced fully by the football association until the 1967/68 season, when they were allowed for tactical reasons. Had Germany just taken out Geoff Hurst at the knees before extra time, we could all be speaking German. Wait …

It isn't surprising, therefore, that the concept of having a bench is a relatively new addition to the fantasy football world. Back when you played your game by post, you just picked 11 players and if one of them didn't start then that was on you. The pressure to field a side guaranteed to play 90 minutes was part of the skill of the game. Fast forward to present day and you are generally afforded four subs (including goalkeeper) to act as a safety net for any last-minute changes. But before your grandad hits you with a coal mining 'when I was a lad', that's not to say it's any easier to get it right! There's a certain reassurance of something being utterly out of your control. Now, you have to wrestle with the weighty decision of who to leave on the bench and who to give the starting spot to. I've found myself on the toilet many a time, audibly having a fictional conversation as I explain to Troy Deeney that I don't fancy him away at Spurs. I could drop Jamie Vardy at home to Chelsea but he would fictionally attack me with a fictional bottle of WKD Blue (other fictional alcopops are available from fictional retailers). The deliberation, however, isn't fictional, far from it.

Not only that, but there's a real difference of opinion on how to manage your bench. Some of your friends, no doubt, like to litter their subs bench with the real dregs of the game. They will filter all positions in price ascending and pick the cheapest players available to them. It's why Jimmy McTavish, a youth player at United wearing squad number '69', will be picked two per cent of the time, despite only coming on to the pitch to fork up the turf at half-time. It's the method the guys from *Geordie Shore* use when buying condoms: he may as well get the cheapest brand because he hopes never to have to use them. This, of course, allows you to spend your riches on the starting line-up and affords you the luxury of not having to carry a 'weaker' player, usually in midfield, every week. It's a legitimate tactic and one that led to one of us having Jermaine Jenas in our squad for an entire season, even though he retired by December and was a pundit by January. The obvious downfall is that it gives you no flexibility week to week on who to start, depending on the opposition. Essentially, you are back playing the 90s version of the game we spoke about earlier, completely dependent on your starting 11, and if you were to explore the squads of the top players online, none of them will have pundits on their bench.

Something that will astound you, for one reason or another, is that some people still don't know their bench is listed in priority order. Many of you will have read that with the eye roll you give people who tell you that a tomato is actually a fruit rather than a vegetable, but I guarantee some people will have read that with the same jaw drop that they had when they heard you could just boil pasta in the kettle to save washing up. I once knew a guy who liked to sort his bench alphabetically, so Aaron Aardvark, for example, was always listed first. That OCD may well have cost him 100 points over the season as everyone knows Aaron Aardvark is terrible away from home, although he does have the nose for a goal. Some players also like to mess with the heads of their mini-league opponents by deliberately starting players who are injured or suspended, so that their total looks lower before the subs are made. As if lulling someone into a false sense of security will make them gung-ho in making early transfers. Maybe Aaron will even get a game. It makes no difference, obviously, but it is some sweet, sweet trolling it has to be said. It's worth having a look at your rivals' benches to see if they know what they're doing and if they don't then for god's sake don't tell them! There's a vacuum cleaner on the line here!

A good fantasy football player will assess fixtures and get their bench in order accordingly. You need to know who scores against whom, what the result was last season, and who keeps clean sheets at home. Tarkowski for Burnley might be a much better pick than Trippier away from home, despite the obvious monetary value difference, and if you don't have a strong bench you can't make those arduous decisions (side note: 'arduous' is actually Aaron Aardvark's middle name). It all becomes utterly inconsequential, of course, by 3:05pm when the guy on your bench scores a forty-yard screamer and all you can do is bitch about it on Twitter. That's the thing about Aaron Arduous Aardvark, he really can hit them.

As you probably know, one of the real holy grails in beating your mates is arming yourself with a back line of the near mythical beast that is the goal-scoring defender. Normally the lesser-spotted prolific defender takes one of two forms. First, there's the old-school aerial threat that gets you excited at every corner and makes you suddenly passionate about the practice of short corners and how much you hate them. Secondly, there's the set-piece maestro who has somehow managed to infiltrate the attackers' alliance and get themselves on penalty duty. Think Denis Irwin or Julian Dicks. Then unthink Julian Dicks, never think of him again, and for god's sake don't say his name five times in the mirror. There is, however, the unthinkable scenario of combining these two breeds and creating the perfect superhuman of a penalty-taking, header-winning goal monster of a defender otherwise known as David Unsworth, who banged in 38 goals in his Premier League career, 22 of which were penalties. Ideally I'd like there to be a Venn diagram below displaying this, and if it isn't there I can only apologise for the lack of budget there must have been to not include what we are now coining 'The Unsworth Conundrum', which sounds like the only episode of *The Big Bang Theory* that wouldn't make me reach for the fusebox.

They aren't just mythical creatures of yesteryear, and with the rise of the ball-playing defender, there's no reason there won't be the opportunity to have four of them in your fantasy line-up. This is where it is helpful to actually watch football. That might sound stupid but most of your workmates will watch *Match of the Day,* maximum, and will only tell you useful sound bytes after. It's easy to know that Marcos Alonso takes free kicks for Chelsea now! He's scored a shed load of them and that's why he's the most expensive defender in every format of the game. However, if you had seen his first season, you will have spotted him gradually muscling his way into the Hazard vs Willian conversation for who gets to take them. *Match of the Day* isn't in the habit of showing missed free kicks. Trent Alexander-Arnold, for example, was someone who was in a good player's squad a long time ago. He broke through in a busy Liverpool side and was comparatively unknown. It is a little-known fact that his first goal for the club came from a free kick against Hoffenheim in a Champions League play-off. He also pulled rank at under-21 level so it might be only a matter of time before he starts to be the go-to guy at Premier League level. All of a sudden he's a free-kick taking full-back with assists in his arsenal, and no one even knows. Also, have a look at the Championship statistics as the season draws to an end. Many a good player has gone unnoticed in August in the Premier League because people dismiss the division's new boys. Anyone who watched any Championship football could've told you that James Maddison was going to be great in a Leicester shirt, and it's a quick way to give yourself a head start in the mini-league. After all, you can't keep picking Julian Dicks.

While consistencies like captains, subs and squad selections are what you need to get you in the title hunt over the 38 game weeks, in my particular experience leagues have been won and lost in the final furlong. That's because in recent years the people behind fantasy football have tried to sex things up with 'chips' or 'special features', like when they put the word 'Turbo' on the end of 'Street Fighter 2' even though it really didn't feel much different. Fantasy Football GTI – that's what we are dealing with. These one-off chips can triple your captain's score, include your bench points or turn a chosen player into a centaur. I think. I don't know, it's hard to keep up sometimes. When and how you use these will often determine whether you end a season in celebration or put your WhatsApp group on mute. Truth be told, they're also the reason some people don't bother, or give up altogether. You knew it was too complicated for your dad when you asked him to get involved back in July. That's why you also took his 20 quid off him in game week one as he asked, 'It's telling me to pick a captain, do I do that with my fingers?' It's this kind of cruel but kind thinking that will give you the mental strength to one day put him in a home. Just remember to set up the direct debit and get his login now, while it still makes sense.

The triple captain is a feature on the most popular version of the game and has led to more online arguments than Piers Morgan wearing an ambiguously coloured dress. Some people will tell you that you have to save it for the 'double game weeks', an anomaly that occurs late in the season when some teams play twice in one point-scoring period, therefore having 180 minutes to have their points tripled. On paper, it makes sense, obviously, to double your chances of points, but it's hardly a science, and if the best striker in the league is at home to the worst defence in the league then why not use it on a single week?

In truth, those extra six points, on a good week, aren't going to win or lose you a league, so leave the obsessing and deliberating to your mates and people who call themselves @FantasyFootballTimeLord on Twitter and have 108 followers. The same sort of obsession exists within the word 'differential', which to you and I means clever picks – the idea of finding someone who scores well but is only owned by 0.1 per cent of people playing. It makes sense that if Mo Salah is owned by everyone in your league then his 17 goals against Watford don't do anything for your league position, and that's often forgotten. At the same time, you don't want to be the only person who *doesn't* own Salah when he scores big. So, the trick is to find spaces for players in your squad who are about to score well while flying under the radar. It could be doubling up on two defenders from the same team or picking a player who will replace a long-term injury and hasn't been selected by the masses yet. Make no mistake, though, describing this as a 'differential' doesn't do anyone any favours, least not those of us trying to defend this as an acceptable hobby for socially adept people. It's like sending your kid into school with a briefcase. It's just digging for gold, it doesn't need a stupid title. Just like those people who order a 'mimosa' and say it's their 'absolute favourite'. It's a Bucks Fizz, mate. You know it. We know it. Wetherspoons know it.

Arguably, the best addition to the game since the retro 90s format is the wildcard – the ability to make as many transfers as you like twice a season stops even the laziest league member giving up, safe in the knowledge that you can wipe the slate clean and start again. You could view your repeated behaviour of making the same mistakes over and over, falling into the same traps and going back to murky untrustworthy characters as a good metaphor for the penal system and how we treat career criminals, but, nahhhh, Romelu Lukaku will come good this time. He's apologised for all the other times, he's really sorry. He's changed, I can feel it. Other than luck, skill and blackmail, the wildcard is without doubt your biggest tool in beating your friends. As long as you're in touching distance of the top, a complete overhaul at the right time can change everything. Firstly, don't be too scared to pull the trigger too early. And I mean as early as week three or four. Let's not kid ourselves, we know when something is shit. We have all given up on a film on Netflix after eight minutes, with zero regard for the three years it probably took to make. It's not our fault we don't like subtitles/films with cars/that guy from *Friends*, they should've been clearer in the one-word title. This is no different. In fact, scrap that, it's very different. A film may cost *someone else* £42m but this decision could cost *you* 20 quid! If you've gone hard on new signings that have taken like a duck to an oil slick and City are rotating way more than you ever expected, then go ahead. Use your wildcard and make a change before it's too late. #FPLEbenezerScrooge. However, make sure you make that decision early. If you are on 18 points by Sunday evening then there's no point waiting until midweek, you may as well hit that WC button now and give yourself six days of glorious tinkering. You may normally do your team on

Friday lunchtime in the office and you'll only have yourself to blame when you've accidentally re-picked seven of the same squad. The wildcard is an excuse to do some legal stalking. Go and look at the best team in the world. That's not a ridiculous superlative, actually go and look at the best team in the world. You can now have that team if you want (give or take some pesky value changes) so use it wisely. Even better, use it before an international break and give yourself a whole fortnight of deliberations. Your bedroom will soon look like Russell Crowe's shed in *A Beautiful Mind* but at least you'll have about three imaginary friends helping you make your decision by then. By far the most satisfying way to use your wildcard, however, is one most of us can only dream: game week 38. Those of you who are trained in utter shithousery will have already worked out why, but for those of you with ethics, I will explain. If you should find yourself top of the league in a title race to the wire then saving that wildcard might be what brings home the title. As soon as game week 37 comes to its conclusion, activate your wildcard and take yourself promptly the squad of your mate in second place. Then it's just a case of ctrl+c, ctrl+v while you make your squad absolutely identical to theirs. They will obviously make their allocated one change, or two if they've been frugal, but that won't be enough to counteract the points difference and the real kicker is they won't have a clue you've done it. You just need to wait until kick-off on the final day and post a screenshot followed by a series of your favourite GIFs and wait for the seethe. It's sneaky, it's sadistic, it's cruel. It's fantasy football.

In fact, if you really are committed to beating your friends then you will need to acknowledge the fact that these 'off-the-field' antics are just as important as your team selection. You're going to need to get involved in some verbal warfare and get in their heads. They let you into their circle of trust in Year 6 when they invited you to their birthday even though you broke their bendy ruler and gave them a religious Christmas card and not a fun cartoon penguin one. Now, decades later, you're going to make them regret it.

If you want to learn from the best then Sir Alex Ferguson was the undisputed king of mind games. I am talking in terms of football, you understand. Charles Manson famously convinced an army of followers that he was some sort of messiah and declared a psychopathic race war to his 'family'. He could probably stake a claim as *the* king of mind games and it is safe to say Dwight Yorke and Andy Cole would've played a far less substantial role in the treble-winning 98/99 season had Manson been at the helm at Old Trafford. Within football, however, Ferguson completely changed the function of a pre-match press conference and football media in general. Simultaneously, he created his own army of managers who realised a game could be won and lost before a ball was kicked and with it a clusterfuck of confusion for the real victims here, fantasy football managers. It's all very well wanting to mess with people's heads yourself, but first you have to navigate those inconvenient real-life managers doing exactly the same to you. Most Premier League manager mind games revolve around the severity or even existence of an injury. Nothing throws you into more chaos than a club boss carelessly throwing out a casual 'Agüero is 50/50 for tomorrow' as if it was nothing. For all we know Agüero is at home on his pogo stick, spinning plates and masturbating, laughing at this private joke, with the full intention of banging in a hat-trick the following morning. But we don't know that! I mean, we're all now picturing that, but we don't *know* that. All of a sudden he's 50/50, you've frantically logged on to your fantasy league, and now your line-up has had more personnel changes than the Sugababes. Leave him in and you face the embarrassing situation of him not playing, scoring zero and walking into work to be reminded by Kevin from accounts that he heard Sergio was 50/50 the day before the game. Kevin tends to regurgitate sound bytes he hears on *Match of the Day* and enlightens you with phrases like 'Belgium could be an underdog for the Euros'. In that very moment, you probably wish that Kevin believed Charles Manson was the messiah, and grew up in California in the late 60s, but for now he is annoyingly right. The alternative, of course, is that you take Agüero out for someone like – but not necessarily – Ayoze Pérez, who scores a bland two points, while everyone else in your mini-league, even those who haven't touched their team in seven weeks, pick up Agüero's inevitable 20-point haul. The lesson here? Don't pay attention to rumours, don't pick someone like – but not necessarily – Ayoze Pérez, and don't join cults.

Let's get to the good bit, though. There's nothing like getting inside the psyche of your mini-league rivals on the group chat. You need to forget the hierarchy of your friendship group and get your hands dirty. It doesn't matter if they're the whipping boy or the quarterback, if you want to win your league then you need to know exactly how to force them into mistakes. First thing's first, no talking football on a Saturday morning or even Friday night. We all love football, mate, but you need to cut that shit out if you want to get to the top. There's nothing worse than someone popping over to your desk on a Friday or, god forbid, if you work on a Saturday, and asking you 'who've you captained?' Firstly, we told you people ask that, didn't we? Secondly, goddamnit, this idiot just reminded everyone in earshot to do their teams! Unacceptable! No one likes the overly nice guy who reveals breaking injury news to the entire group on a weekend. If you want injury news, create a Google alert, if you want to make friends, fuck off to Parkrun, Steve! To be honest, this doesn't just apply to football chat, I wouldn't say anything at all until that deadline passes. You might think commenting on this week's *Bake Off* is innocent, but the warped mind of a fantasy football addict can see that as a reminder, quick smart. Bake off. Challenges. Technical Challenge. Technical Area. Football. Deadline! It's as easy as that. The six degrees of fantasy football is a much easier game than Kevin Bacon and it will only end in you being condemned by all your friends. Forcing your friends to miss deadlines is mind games 101 and should really be par for the course in even the most civil of mini-leagues. Unless you're up against a Mormon brotherhood or Peter Andre then everyone should really be living by that principle. Something that might not come as easy to you is gloating. We spend our whole lives being taught to be humble but there's no place for that here. A friend of mine recently told us he missed the Saturday morning deadline because his young daughter was watching Disney's *Moana* on his iPad. He was looking for sympathy and what he received was 423 screen shots from Disney's *Moana* in a variety of compromising situations within a one-hour period. You *chose* to have children Damien, and therefore you aren't taking this as seriously as I am. There's nothing worse than someone being smug over a lucky game week where they top scored, and the fact it winds us all up so much is exactly why you should do it too. It causes people to react or do something stupid. The more original and obnoxious your boasting can get, the better. One stand-out story from one of our listeners over the years was an incredible slow play personal attack over the festive period. Riding high in his league, *Mr X* – as we'll refer to him, to protect the innocent – decided to hit his closest adversary where it hurts. No, not his bad dress sense in the 90s or even his onset diabetes, he went for the jugular and got his family involved. As he opened his mail one December morning, among many traditional Christmas cards we have all seen many times before, he gets an offering from Mr X. He could spot the smug handwriting anywhere. As he slowly pulled out the card like Charlie Bucket would a chocolate bar, his face dropped as he realised it was a full family photo in front of the tree with Mr X and his wife and children. No, I mean *his* wife and children. Mr Runner-up's own wife had betrayed him, posing with festive jumpers and a 'Fantasy Football Champion 2016' sign held proudly by Mr X as he embraced children that weren't his. Sure, one of the kids wasn't Mr Runner-up's either but that's a story for a different time and why these people have been kept anonymous. That's the level we are talking about here though, the lengths people will go to in order to gain any form of advantage. God only knows where team selection ranked in Mr Runner-up's list of priorities that game week. He probably captained Christian Benteke and converted to Judaism. Anything not to look at that abomination of a card. Some take digs and jibes to a different level entirely and don't even need family members to be present when they're planning a personal attack. One fantasy football player tweeted about a prank in his head-to-head league, with zero fucks given, that his opponent's father had recently passed away, so he had messaged him to say he was 'sorry for his loss'. He then waited all of two minutes and messaged a screenshot of their head-to-head matchup with the caption 'sorry for your other loss'. Now we aren't condoning exploiting dead relatives, but it might make you realise your taunts of 'wally' and 'stupidhead' might not be as cutting as you once thought.

Any forum in which you can communicate with your league mates is as important a tool as any of your in-game features. A well-timed goad can be just as fruitful as a transfer or a wildcard. Most of this, obviously, goes down in the WhatsApp group, the group chat, the thing on your phone that makes you miss an entire scene from *Game of*

Thrones but you don't want to admit it to your other half so you just pretend you still know what's going on and hope to god you didn't miss one of the weirdly sexy incest bits. Back in the 90s you would be in a fantasy football league with your colleagues and it would make those office hours more bearable as you goaded each other and looked at the league table on the staffroom noticeboard. These days, however, you get to play fantasy football with people you actually like, so you don't do it in silence. God no, you message each other constantly. To be honest, on the fifth or sixth video of penguin dancing or Zorb football leg breaks, I often forget there was a reason for the WhatsApp group in the first place. It's an open space, a trust tree where you can say anything, safe in the knowledge you will be crucified for it, but privately. Unless, of course you use the word 'banter' unironically, in which case you can consider yourself ejected immediately. But most importantly, it is for revelling and revenge in equal measure and there's a whole arsenal of tricks that can get in your friends' heads. I particularly like the subtle, slow played digs that could easily just pass for conversation, but the doubt hits them later at their desk like a tranquiliser dart. Americans would call it 'trash talk' but we much prefer the term 'psychological warfare', and here are five of my favourite rival-baiting classics that I implore you to use whenever possible:

1. 'The league is basically yours to lose.'

An absolute mainstay of the fantasy football group chat, usually said to the league leader in about late August to get under their skin and make them try to be clever. They will fend it off at first, but if you can get the other league members to join in they will eventually believe their own hype. It will also create this weird mentality where they almost *want* to lose to prove to you that they aren't infallible and hit you with the most confusing 'I told you so' that ever existed. On that note, don't be shy of lobbying for other league members to get stuck in away from the group chat, but beware of the *second* group chat. the one that excludes the runt of the litter and discusses how shit he or she is and laughs at their captaincy choices behind their back. If your league doesn't have a breakaway WhatsApp group then I'm sorry you had to find out like this … but you're the runt.

2. 'I know who you're going to captain anyway.'

A late Friday night assault delivered to the person directly above you in the league. They'll almost certainly change their mind 17 times in the next five minutes, largely about whether you are coming to their wedding anymore. Totally worth it. It's the stick or swap at the end of *Deal or No Deal* multiplied by 1,000. I remember hearing a story in which Alan Shearer approached fellow 90s Premier League striking stalwart Matt Le Tissier just before Le Tis was about to take a penalty for Southampton against Shearer's Newcastle. Shearer said something along the lines of 'stick it to the left'. Now, what Shearer did was quite ingenious really, because it would have made Le Tissier think twice. He was sewing a seed of doubt. What did Shearer know? *Should* he stick the penalty to the left? Was that what the keeper was expecting? Should he put it to the right? Was he double-bluffing him? Was it the old covert triple-bluff? Obviously, the crafty Geordie was just messing with Le Tissier and knew nothing other than the fact that saying 'stick it to the left' would make Le Tissier panic and have him thinking and guessing right up until the point he was about to take the penalty. However, Le Tis scored 47 of 48 penalties as a Southampton player, and that solo miss did not come against Newcastle. There's literally no way upon hearing 'I know who you're going to captain anyway' that you don't login into your team and at least consider that you might have made the wrong call. Worst case scenario is they get it right and you say 'knew you would. Good shout, well played', making them wonder whether you were being sincere the whole time. Best case is they flip-flop between their two options so much they go absolutely rogue and captain their keeper and put tin foil on their head and go full 2007 Britney.

3. 'Any proper football fan knows that …'

This can be followed by literally any old shite. Zaha loves playing on a wide pitch, Giroud's best games come away from home in London, Adam Lallana never performs on his daughter's birthday. Does he have a daughter? Don't know. Doesn't matter. It's such a character assassination and attack of the most territorial nature, you may as well have pissed in their garden while getting off with their other half. This one can be delivered at any point, even when not talking about fantasy football. It will worm its way into their line-up, don't you worry. Such an arrogant level of football snobbery won't bother anyone who really does know their onions, but anyone with the tiniest of chips on their shoulder will get defensive almost instantly. They might even look up some useless nonsense and hit you back with a fact or stat, to which you can just give them the old 'Yeah, I guess it's different when you only see games on TV. Maybe you're right.' They will start to try and find that connoisseur's gem in the database of players and we both know they won't find him.

4. 'I see you've brought (insert player) in. That's brave.'
You will instantly be met with a 'why?' This will be followed by increasingly aggressive questioning techniques and demands for explanations. This is because you will not reply to the messages under any circumstances. They will unravel into all sorts of ill-informed decisions and self-doubt. If there's a member of your league who suffers with paranoia or an anxiety disorder then, of course, that's perfect! That's your guy! Their instinct will be that you know something they don't, like an injury, criminal proceedings or South Korean military service. No one wants to be the guy who stupidly brought in Darron Gibson right before he got lifted for drink driving. I mean, no one wants to be the guy who brought in Darron Gibson as a teetotal cyclist, but you get the picture. Their hunt for information will be utterly futile and the only thing they will discover is that they really are starting to wonder why you are even friends.

5. 'I'm very much the underdog anyway.'

It is very important that you make everyone aware you are not a threat. This can be backed up by fake holidays and imaginary work deadlines where you claim you might not even be able to change your team. 'I'm going away to Cornwall for a week in September. Signal will be a nightmare so that's me in trouble.' A simple little lie will lower expectations among your rivals. They will see any score lower than yours that week as a real embarrassment. You do obviously have to really commit to this bit. Limited messages, photos of Cornwall, live like a hermit. The usual. Don't fully commit and *actually* go to Cornwall though as the signal truly will be terrible. Throughout the season, scatter in self-deprecating performance reviews just by adding the word 'even' here and there. 'Even *I* got my captain choice right this week.' 'Even *I* knew Kane was back fit.' 'Even *I* knew about the early kick-off and I'm in Cornwall.' It will have little effect on their actual fantasy performance but it is bloody tremendous if you beat them come the end of the season.

Finally, if you're dead set on beating your mates then you can always get new mates! That's not as ridiculous as it sounds, I promise. There's no limit to the number of leagues you can join so play the numbers game and be the best in as many as you can. I never liked my old school friends meeting my work friends as the only thing they'll initially have in common is me and they'll likely talk about me. I know, it's a control thing, I should see someone. So, I keep them separate, not only in life but in fantasy leagues too. If you are struggling in one league with a few guys who seem to always do well then use them. Suck out all their knowledge and use it so that you are better in the weaker leagues. In the land of the blind, the one-eyed man is king, so who cares if you are the whipping boy in one, but the king in the other four, especially if there is money at stake! Also, if you are able to use your position at work to your advantage then do it. My boss once called me in for a verbal warning disciplinary meeting. It genuinely got me worried as I had no idea what they were on about and I had to defend myself against some bullshit accusations. It wasn't until the meeting had finished that he explained he just wanted to keep me busy until the deadline had passed to set your team. It was brilliant. We were work friends not real friends, and he knew the difference. You should also do your best to not have the same people in multiple leagues, unless, of course, you know they're terrible. There's nothing worse than coming second to the same guy in about five different leagues and worse still having to hand over money at the end of the season. You've got to play the odds and give yourself the best chance, so suggesting your mates to fill spots in small leagues isn't smart business. Don't see 'there's only four of us in there, it's our first proper season doing it and Juan can't even read English. It's twenty quid per person, is that OK?' as a bad thing. That's a great thing! You don't need 15 teams to make a good league. You just made yourself the easiest 60 notes ever and Juan will learn English the hard way, when he sees a Christmas card with you and his wife kissing under the mistletoe.

One final duplicitous step you can take if you want to garner an advantage over your nearest and dearest is the biggest of all fantasy football taboos. Create a second team. It's 100 per cent against the rules and you even have to create a second email address, which for some of us is the closest we will get to being in MI5. This secret sausage team can act as a blueprint for all the things you wanted to do but didn't have the balls. If you had a hunch that Watford's 14th manager of the season will have plans that get the best out of their new attacking midfielder then you can try it in your secret team. If it works then you can take it from test phase to the real deal. It's like practising kissing or sex with your cousin, only illegal. You can give the team a really meta name or a taunting anagram or Latin translation just to rub it in the faces of authorities, like you're Hannibal Lecter desperate to get caught, but you shouldn't actually join any mini-leagues. Anonymity is everything. This isn't one to talk about in the group chat or in fact to anyone. Firstly, it's against the rules and the website will genuinely shut down your team. Secondly, it's frankly embarrassing that any of us are going to this length to win a fictional football competition that is already causing a strain on your relationship with your children, and that was when you were 'managing' just one team. The truth is, you'll never know if any of your friends are doing this but if it helps you win then who cares? It was worth it.

I'm Just Unlucky

ONTRARY to popular belief, hindsight is *not* a wonderful thing, it is, in fact, an utterly useless thing. The sort of thing that can slowly grind you down and destroy your life. Imagine if Gareth Southgate had the hindsight to stick his Euro '96 semi-final penalty to the keeper's left. Imagine if Ryan Giggs had the hindsight to say, 'Sorry, bro, I'm busy tonight, I can't come over and meet your new girlfriend'. Hindsight is also why we are certain that everyone who has ever played fantasy football has, at one point, daydreamed about having a time machine. I mean, that's probably a bold statement and we haven't spoken to *everyone* who has ever played fantasy football, but we are pretty confident that these thoughts have gone through the minds of gaffers across the globe when a defender that is 0.2 per cent picked gets two goals, an assist, a clean sheet and maximum bonus points. We've all glazed over as the final whistle is blown, imagining that we'd had the aforementioned hindsight to not only include said fictional, underappreciated defender in our teams, but to have put the captain's armband on him and watch his colossal game-week points double. Get in the time machine! We've all pictured leaning nonchalantly on the fruit machine in the pub, inspecting the fingernails on your left hand while casually sipping a pint, as friends, acquaintances and strangers gather around to bask in your excellence while you regale to them that you 'just had a feeling' the fifth-choice Southampton centre-back had a brace in him, away from home against Chelsea.

Let's be honest, if there was such a thing as an *actual* time machine, what sort of lunatic would squander its powers to be better at fantasy football instead of going back in time and selecting the winning EuroMillions lottery numbers? Or whizzing back to the early 90s and knocking on the door of Bloomsbury Publishing with the *Harry Potter* books in a briefcase? The thing is, I know for a fact that I've definitely had more lucid fantasies about going back *just* far enough in time to select an out-of-form Nicklas Bendtner an hour and a half before he scores a couple of hugely surprising wonder goals than I have about matching that seventh little numbered ball and my life changing forever. But what is more important in life, beating your mates in your mini-league or being a multi-millionaire? I mean it's being a multi-millionaire, isn't it? Well, for any normal person it probably is. But when fantasy football fever takes over, managers aren't normal people. Rational, stable human beings, usually capable of successfully holding down conversations and carrying out the usual weekend tasks – sometimes even at the same time – become obsessive, agitated, zombies focused on nothing but feasting on fantasy football. It's our chance to become the football manager we all believe we have within us, ever since it was your turn to pick your team in PE. Yeah, you picked your best mate first, but after that, everyone else was fair game. You needed to be shrewd and pick the disinterested kid who would be happy to play in goal before the opposition did, otherwise the rest of your team would be left arguing over who went between the sticks. Ultimately, you'd give up completely and decide you had to play rush-goalie, which was the most unsuccessful footballing decision since Stuart Pearce stuck David James upfront for Man City. Seriously, look it up! No one even wanted to get back and be rush-goalie, so every time your team conceded, which they inevitably always would, it would be *all* of your faults and you all knew it. No, you needed to pick the lad who brought his own lab coat to science lessons before you started choosing between the other dozen boys who fancied themselves as decent strikers. From the day you realised this incredibly important fact, you became an internal manager, secretly confident you could do a better job than 90 per cent of the managers you would come across for the rest of your life.

It's something we never lose. It's the guy who screams in anger at the TV so ferociously his dog shits himself and runs up the stairs. It's the 25-stone bloke on his eighth pint, a Spurs shirt stretched over his enormous belly as the barstool screams in agony beneath him, who referred to Lampard as 'Fat Frank' and claimed he's lost a yard or two. We all think we know our football, and this is the closest most of us will ever get, unless you decide to start up an under-10's Sunday league team, but who needs the hassle of that? Surely if you want to be threatened by aggressive, competitive parents who feel that you've been unfair towards their fantastically gifted child, you'd take up teaching in a private school.

But fantasy football has it's lucky and unlucky moments and you'll be able to put most of the hideous things that happen to you down to the latter. That's what it is. It's not your fault, it's because the fantasy gods have taken a particular dislike to you this game week. Or perhaps the reason you've barely broken double figures for the last fortnight isn't because of your lack of talent and skill at the game, it's probably just karma for the time you accidentally tried to wipe that girl's birthmark off her face because you thought it was chocolate. Yeah, that's all it is, the universe has just got it in for you this month. Next time it'll be better.

However, no matter how much you convince yourself that it's not your fault, there are several scenarios where your own stupidity and naivety can't be blamed on unluckiness, voodoo, black magic or Donald Trump.

Is there a better feeling than the pure, unadulterated relief of waking up in the morning and thinking for a split second that you have to get out of your warm bed and go to work, before realising it is, in fact, Saturday? You stretch, flip the pillow over to the cold side and fall back to sleep with a smile on your face. There's going to be a definite spring in your step for the rest of the day. Perhaps you stay in bed a little while once you finally do wake from your glorious lie-in. Maybe you flick the telly on and daydream about finally going on *Dragons' Den* with your multi-million-pound idea of a fry-up delivery service, which, by the way, is absolutely genius. The only problem would be keeping the fried eggs warm. Unless the driver cooked them in the back of the car on a portable hob once he'd pulled up to the house. Yes, that's it. Literally *cracked* it. Get me in front of Peter Jones, Deborah Meaden and the one who looks like Theo Paphitis but isn't Theo Paphitis.

And then you realise – your daydreaming is interrupted by a sudden, colossal punch to your solar plexus as the realisation hits you like Adebayo Akinfenwa going two footed into a kiddies' ball-pit – you didn't set your fantasy football team! You reach for your phone, you fumble, wincing, praying there's time. There must be time! But alas, you have made one of the cardinal sins of fantasy football. It is 11:47. It is too late. All is lost.

Damn you comfortable bed and *Saturday Kitchen Live*! Why had you waited so long to set the line-up? You knew what you were going to do by Tuesday lunchtime. Somehow, you've managed to be both an overly cautious fool and a carefree idiot with no real grasp of responsibility. If only you had been at work this morning, you would have got out of bed and set your line-up before you'd even had your cornflakes. God, you wish you worked on Saturdays! Your lackadaisical ways have tainted the lie-in, the bed now feels dirty, the cold pillow is like failure, the *Saturday Kitchen*

Live presenters seem to be mocking you as they eat their braised salmon and drink their white wine at 11.48am.

What state had you left your team in? How bad was it? Without looking, we can probably tell you: the in-form player with the great fixture is second on your bench. You'll be starting the guy who is going to get a four-minute run around at the very end of the game like some kind of competition winner. The player who is likely to concede five is, of course, starting and the captain's armband is on your attacking midfielder who is playing in a holding role this weekend because of an injury to their usual defensive-midfielder (also in your team). This is how fantasy football works. This is how the fantasy football gods punish us for our mistakes. There's also the added kick in the balls that you were going to transfer in the little fella who plays up front for Southampton, but didn't, and he will undoubtedly score at least two goals to rub your face in it. It's an absolute bloody certainty. It is always the way. In fact, it's *such* a dead cert that maybe you could turn it around a little bit, maybe save the weekend. You should soften the blow of forgetting to set your team by putting a bet on the little fella at Southampton to get that brace. Yeah, great idea. He's bound to score, so go lump a few quid on it. Perfect. Maybe just a little snooze first though, hey.

The virtues of sleep, even when it's unwanted, can't save you from a glaring, dare I say *evil*, glitch that appears in one particular incarnation of the fantasy football game. 'Glitch' probably isn't the right word, as that alludes to the fact that it is a mistake or something that has been overlooked, whereas this particular quirk is no accident. This malevolence is very much intentional. When a player has played for 60 minutes and the opposition team hasn't scored, he is awarded with additional points for obtaining a clean sheet. Goalkeepers and defenders get four points each and a midfielder gets one. Sounds fine, right? Right?

You see, if you're anything more than a mere fair weather, casual fantasy football manager who can't always remember his login details and isn't overly fussed how he does, then you will refresh your team's points several hundred times during a Saturday. That's the law. Even when you know the final whistle was blown in the late kick-off ten minutes ago, you're still refreshing in case you missed something, or, more likely, the website did.

There will be one particular refresh – I like to call it the *reBest* – where your points total will suddenly skyrocket. A dozen or more points will have suddenly been added to your total in one tap of that little bendy refresh arrow. God bless that little bendy refresh arrow. You see, what has happened is you have hit the 60th minute, the hour mark, that holy grail for sometimes even doubling game-week scores. The 60th minute is a natural phenomenon, very much like a rainbow, the Northern Lights or Wayne Rooney's regenerating hair. But the problem with being awarded these points is that you have 30 minutes to hold on to those points, 30 long minutes for it all to go wrong. There is still a third of the game to go and there's no cash-out option. But as far as you are concerned, those points are yours, they're in the bag, a done deal. If it was metaphorical money, in your mind it would be spent. You've probably screenshat (past tense of screenshot) your huge score and smugly posted it in your mini-league WhatsApp group. Maybe you've tweeted the picture along with a few flame emojis and that little smiley face with hearts for eyes. Maybe you emailed the picture of the obscene score to yourself, printed it off and popped it in the post to your Year 7 maths teacher who told you that you would never amount to anything.

Unfortunately, what you are doing is counting your chickens. I've never understood where that phrase came from. I can only assume that there once must have been an unorthodox farmer somewhere who owned both chickens and wolves and had a bloody nightmare on stocktake day. Every time he counted, there was one less. But then again, he should have been pretty happy to have bred wolf-eating chickens in the first place.

If you're lucky, the inevitable goal that wipes out your clean sheet and, as a result, all your beautiful, glorious points, comes sooner rather than later. I've personally experienced a 62nd minute soiling of my fresh-smelling, crisp clean sheet. While it was still a blow, the nine points I lost as the result of a single goal were only mine for a mere two minutes. I hadn't really had time to process them, or swim around in them like Scrooge McDuck in his vault of gold, they were there one minute (61 minutes) and gone the next (62 minutes). I certainly hadn't had time to gloat. It was for the best. I knew it at the time. If it was going to happen, better then than in injury time. I've witnessed clean sheet wipe-outs at 96 minutes – six minutes into injury time! By then your wolf-eating chickens are plucked, gutted and in a casserole ready for dinner, let alone just counted. It's enough to make you crazy. It's the ultimate 'this is what you could have won' scenario.

There are also other pitfalls with clean-sheet points. Let us not forget, friends, the colossal arseache of your defender, on a clean sheet, being substituted at 59 minutes – 59 MINUTES?! Now, that is the move – *dick* move, might I add – of a manager who knows his best mate has that defender in his fantasy football team and is doing it to wind him up and gain some ground in their mini-league. Why else would he take him off at 59 minutes? At least keep him on for the hour, maybe even give the lad 70 minutes to run around, but 59? I don't know which is worse, knowing that your player was less than 60 seconds away from an additional four points or having those four points ripped from your hands on the 90-minute mark.

It's not just clean-sheet shaped chickens that can be swiped from underneath your nose. What about the player who decides to give away a penalty in the last minute of the game, subsequently getting a red card and ending the week on zero, if not *minus* points. Or how about owning the player who's about to *take* the last-minute penalty? That's great news, isn't it? You thought you were done for the game week, but no, in a rare turn of form and luck you're actually going to *benefit* from a huge last-minute decision, the final kick of the ball is going to be a positive for you, and your 48 points for the week should be a punishing 55 when this goes in. Ah, no, of course. Your player, the same one that Jonathan Pearce assured you would almost certainly score because of his 'impeccable record from the spot', did, in fact, miss. The 48 points now goes down to 46, but if he'd have scored, you were looking at points for the goal and maybe even a bonus or two, so technically that miss has actually cost you ten points. Ten points because he can't score a goal from 12 yards! On the amount of money *he's* on!

The moral of this brief story of despair, frustration and petrifying chickens that would need to be about seven feet tall if they were able to feasibly eat a fully grown wolf is probably not to hit the refresh button too often. If you logged into your fantasy football team at the very end of the day, once the dust had settled and all the points were accounted for, then there would be none of the vanishing points, none of the 'what ifs', none of the 'if onlys', and no attempts to break into letterboxes to retrieve premature hate mail for octogenarian maths teachers. But then where's the fun in that?

Ultimately, we are only human and you will, of course, make these mistakes. It's natural to oversleep, and it's nigh-on impossible not to grant yourself a little peek at your score before the final whistle blows. But because you have acknowledged your own mortality and limitations, and, as a result, your *failings*, it's the things that are out of your control that hurt the most. The universe does like to throw various spanners into the works and these spanners come in many disguises. For instance, the dreaded international break.

If you'd have said to me in the balmy summer of 1996 that in my adult life I would feel so indifferent about an England game that I won't even bother watching it, then I would have cried into my Kellogg's Banana Bubbles. The reason is partly down to the fact that the England national team are quite simply not as likeable as they were back in the day. The David Seamans, Stuart Pearces, Paul Inces and Gazzas of the 90s were replaced by the John Terrys, Ashley Coles and Wayne Rooneys of the 00s, and eventually the Jamie Vardys, Ashley Youngs and Jack Wilsheres of nowadays. The other, larger, contributing factor to the impending dread that an international break brings with it like an unwelcome shadow of shite, is that there's no Premier League football (*real* football) and, as a result, no fantasy footy. What are we supposed to do with all the spare time we have now that we don't have to tinker with our teams? Talk to people? Read a book? Do some *actual* work when we're sat at our desks?

Don't let your boredom and frustration at the lack of real football be your downfall, though, there is the danger of pulling the trigger on a transfer too soon. Even in international friendlies players have a tendency to get injured, and I'm not saying there's a conspiracy or anything, but it always tends to happen roughly 12 seconds after I have just clicked on the 'confirm transfer' button and brought them into my team. As I say, I'm not into conspiracies, but I'm pretty sure it's something to do with Jay Z and that sign he makes with his hands when he's on stage.

The international break is nothing but a hindrance, an inconvenience. Essentially, it's the health and safety officer, probably called Clive, who comes swanning into the laboratory uninvited while you, an important scientist, are busy working on a cure for a terrible disease, telling you there's a fire drill and that you need to get out. 'I don't care even if it *is* just a drill and there's no real danger, that's the rules.' 'No! I'm busy. I can't stop. Leave me alone and let me carry on with my research. People will die!'

The old club versus country debate will forever rage on in football. Some will always be England fans first and support their club second and some will correctly view it the other way around. Likewise, some players will be more synonymous with their national team and remain a mainstay for years and years, while they flit from club to club like a fickle, money-grabbing whore with no sense of loyalty or what is right.

Gary Lineker will always be more of an England player than anything else, maybe because he scored so many impressive and important goals and helped steer the nation to the World Cup semi-final at Italia '90, or maybe because he was wearing an England shirt when he pooped his pants on the telly. Who knows? One thing we do know is that, as a fantasy football manager, the international break isn't a welcome one. It isn't one that is greeted with the glee of a Bank Holiday away from the office. It isn't a chance to forget about fantasy football for a week and do something else. That's not what we want. That's not what we do. And to make things worse, there's football on the TV, there's football happening, it's just not the *right* football. It's a two-bob imitation. It's there to taunt us, like alcohol-free beer or the rubbish softcore movies that used to be on late night on Channel 5. It's not quenching the thirst that is brought on by the lack of proper football, it's making that thirst more evident, more intense. I'm dehydrated, get me a Lucozade, and the one that's like orange squash, not the fizzy one that tastes like medicine.

Sure, there's versions of fantasy football for international tournaments, but who can really play those properly? Once you've spent all your money on the big-name players from the top nations, you have four million quid left to buy two defenders, two midfielders and a budget striker and only have Japan, Saudi Arabia, Algeria and the countries ending in 'stan' to choose from. Either we're watching the Premier League and playing the true fantasy football or we're moaning about the Premier League not being on and that there's no fantasy football to play. It's all incredibly simple, really.

Even though it is often considered the biggest division in the world, the Premier League can be pretty insular like that. Some fans and followers of Premier League football will often only know those players who play in England's top flight. Ask these particular fans to name the full Watford squad and they'll give it a good go, but ask them to name the starting 11, or even just a handful, of Ajax or PSG players and they'll struggle. It's probably why the English are notoriously lazy when it comes to learning another language – we feel we just don't need to. Why do we need to know about other teams in other leagues when we're fully immersed in the 20 teams battling it out week in week out in the mighty Prem.

However, after a big international tournament like the World Cup or Euros, the same blinkered, idle fans suddenly become transnational football gurus. They've sat in front of their telly and watched a hell of a lot of football over the summer and picked up a few nuggets that they believe are theirs, that only they have picked up on. 'Hey, that Mbappé lad is gonna be decent, mark my words.'

It's the same scenario when that kind of fan watches the Championship play-offs. They'll notice a couple of talented lads that will be debuting in the Premier League next season that they'd never heard of before – even though they'd netted 30 goals in the Championship throughout the season and been on most people's radars for ages – and pass them off as *their* discovery. Like they're the scout who spotted them on a dogshit-strewn Sunday at Hackney Marshes. 'Ryan Sessegnon's the one to watch this season, trust me.' It's just passing off information real football fans already knew. You're late to the party with old information, mate. It's like the middle-aged bloke at the office who tells you that he's heard of a pretty groovy new singer called Edward Sheeran who is definitely worth keeping an eye out for.

I used to know a fella who would watch the football in the pub and spend the entire duration of the match making stupid jokes and shouting 'shoot!' every time the keeper was taking a goal kick before laughing uncontrollably at his own awful, *awful* jokes, only to then repeat, verbatim, everything that the pundits said afterwards. He would pass off little nuggets he'd heard like, 'Well, England's problem was that they weren't playing with enough width', as if he actually knew about football and wasn't just there to attempt to make everyone laugh. Luckily he's dead now, so that is some comfort.

The unadulterated joy at the return of the real football after a tournament or even just a week off is truly remarkable for many. But there's a lot of admin to clear up. Some players in your fantasy team could have played twice during the break, which means they are in danger of being rested when returning to club football in favour of someone who isn't good enough to get picked for their country but is well rested. During international duty, your players also had 180 minutes worth of opportunity for them to get injured. That's all the international break is to you, the discerning fantasy football manager, a minefield that your boys have to navigate successfully in order to remain fit for the proper football, and more specifically your fantasy team.

Jaundice, Homer Simpson, lemons, the other characters from *The Simpsons* … did I say lemons? All these things are yellow and lovely (apart from jaundice). Something that is definitely yellow and *not* lovely is when you log into your fantasy football team to see that one of them has picked up an injury and has gone yellow! This very simple yet alarming colour system is specific to the fantasy Premier League version of the game, and the mere hint of yellow on a phone or laptop screen can reduce a grown fantasy football manager to tears, meaning that they too probably start feeling a little under the weather and will soon be a doubt for the weekend as well. There are no overreactions when it comes to the yellowness of a player's status though, it is incredibly worrying. He's picked up an ominous 'knock' (what even is a *knock*?) and is now only 75 per cent likely to play. It's decent odds – if you heard you had a 75 per cent chance with Margot Robbie or 75 per cent chance of winning the lottery, you'd be over the moon, but to see one of your starting 11 has gone yellow and is now *only* 75 per cent likely to play is a different kettle of custard. Suddenly the 25 per cent unlikeliness seems more intimidating than the 75 per cent likeliness. Somehow, there's been some kind of cosmic shift in the universe and for this week only the 25 per cent chance of your player not playing actually outweighs the much larger 75 per cent chance that he *will* play. This kind of talk is like foreplay to Rachel Riley, and I would know, apparently I've got a 25 per cent chance with her.

The conundrum is what to do with said yellow player. Do you chance it? Is the canary-like colour of his current health likely to stop him playing at all, or *even worse* does it mean he'll get a measly 15 minutes and therefore an even measlier one point? Oooh, it's a minefield of possible balls-ups, indecision and regret. Is the potential injured status just manager mind games? José Mourinho is notorious for baiting his rival managers and teasing an injury to key players, only for it to be revealed that the player is, in fact, fine and subsequently goes on to score a hat-trick. This textbook piece of Mourinho mindgamery has had me shaking my fist at my laptop screen on several occasions.

Researching the sources of any injury update is key to finding out whether the yellowness is likely to fade before kick-off, or whether it will evolve into a deep orange, or, as I prefer to think of it, African sunset (50 per cent chance of playing) or turn to full-on redness (gutted, mate – this geezer is FUCKED).

Whether your player is just a little yellow – maybe he sneezed once at training on Tuesday and the boss is keeping an eye on him – or he's gone as red as an embarrassed Phil Mitchell on a frosty bonfire night in Albert Square, you need to pay attention and take action. Maybe the action you take is to not take any action at all, and if that is indeed the action you decide to take then well done; at least action was taken and you took action. Yellow can be dismissed, you're probably not going to transfer out a player who has gone yellow if he holds a regular starting place in your team and is part of a bigger, season-long plan. You can always stick with him and hope that if he doesn't play at all and that the man on your bench replacing him does the business. The second that 75 per cent chance drops to a 50/50 St Tropez glow, then it's time to have a long hard scroll through suitable replacements. Has someone gone full-on Heinz tomato soup orange and ended up playing? Yes. In fact it's a phenomenon that occurs a few times a season. It's not as frequent as, let's say, Graeme Souness getting so angry about a player's haircut that he looks as if he's going to pull his own testicles off in protest, but that one time it happens to you will stay with you for a while. You won't want to be duped by the mis-information again – you'll be defiant in its face, even. When you realise that the orange player you got rid of not only played but *scored*, it'll be the angriest anyone has been with a colour since I watched 'An Evening with the Boyband Blue' at Butlins, Bognor Regis. Utterly seething.

Red, however, is a different beast. Red will often mean a suspension, there's fact behind the absence, and there's a definite return date. Red is honest. It's saying, 'he quite literally will not be available to play until this date. He's at home with his wife, or at least at a team-mate's home with theirs.' Red could also, of course, mean a more serious injury. The player has been medically ruled out until at least a certain date. Perhaps said player is under the surgeon's knife as you click on his profile to see when he'll be back. That information is a little more dubious. You know it won't be in the next few weeks if he's being operated on. Legend has it that suffering a stroke didn't stop Winston Churchill from going into work later that very same day. That's British determination for you. I too have had a stroke in the morning and still made it into work a few hours later, but I don't want to be praised for it, it's just what I do. But whichever way you look at it, a player having surgery won't be around for a while, so regardless of how key he has been in your side and how much you'll need him when he gets back to fitness, you'd better get rid. A two-game suspension or a couple of weeks out with a hammy is fine, you can excuse someone for keeping faith and a seat on the bench for him, but if he has a *lengthy* leave of absence and you don't drop that chump like a hot-shit sandwich, his price is going to plummet and you'll be in all sorts of bother.

You have never known pain until you have transferred in a player, only for him to turn yellow the next day. You spend days checking up on him, seeing if his colour begins to evolve and take on an orangey hue. You feel like Florence Nightingale as you get up in the middle of the night to log in to your team and check up on him. You wish you were actually there, delicately dabbing his sweating brow with a cool flannel and helping him drink water by lamplight. You'll look online for any update on his injury status, googling him dozens of times every hour, looking on the official club website, the online sports sites, the back pages of the tabloids, that bloke on Twitter who reckons he knows Razor Ruddock's agent. You just need to know if he'll be alright, and by alright you clearly mean whether he's going to play the full 90 minutes because you just got rid of Raheem Sterling for him!

Any period of uncertainty is hell for a fantasy football manager. You're not being spoon-fed the facts like the actual managers, who have the luxury of technical staff, physios and doctors at their beck and call. Fantasy football is a one-person game. You're in this on your own, son. We don't have anyone holding our hand and providing us with information to make our decision making easier. We have to believe in our own judgement, and if we're wrong then we have to, quite nobly, blame it on the fact that we don't have the luxury of technical staff, physios and doctors at our beck and call like those other wet wipes. The only time that is more disconcerting than a period of uncertainty is a very specific period of time in late December, which I don't mind declaring as the single most difficult time in any fantasy football manager's calendar, no, scratch that, in a fantasy football manager's *life*. The Christmas fixtures.

I love Christmas. There's no joke here. I have a very real, deep, intense love for Christmas that stems from childhood. In fact, I love Christmas so much I despise anyone who refers to it as 'Xmas' as I feel that it cheapens the day and makes it seem a lot more flippant and less important than it is. But as this book is called *The A-Z of Fantasy Football*, I'll be buggered if I can think of something else that represents the letter X other than maybe some convoluted paragraph about how notorious sicknote Andy Carroll is now more X-ray machine than man. In fact, I still have a long-held tradition of not masturbating on Christmas Day. It just doesn't feel right. It's a holy day, a day for family, love, warmth and, to be honest, I tried it once in my teens and kept picturing Jesus in a party hat looking disappointed at me as he blew out his birthday candles, and I just couldn't continue. It really put me off.

Christmas for most of us consists of eating, drinking and sleeping too much and then moaning about where the time went; you spent it eating, drinking and sleeping too much! But can we please spare a thought for those who are less fortunate at Christmas. Yes, that's right, the footballers. The Christmas fixtures schedule is crazy! It's more chock-a-block than the Vicar of Dibley's mouth during the Brussels sprout-eating competition with David Houghton – and if you don't get that absolute British yuletide constitution of a reference then I don't want to know you. It's not uncommon for players to have a game on Christmas Eve, Boxing Day and New Year's Eve or Day. There's no obscene amount of mince pies and mulled wine for them on 25 December; they're back out there the very next day having to run around for 90 minutes whilst being watched by millions of people across the globe. Granted they get paid tens of thousands of pounds a minute, but that's not the point; imagine not being able to drink bread sauce directly out of the dish on Christmas Day. Imagine it!

Someone else who doesn't have it easy during the Christmas fixture bedlam is a fantasy football manager. Well, more specifically, fantasy football managers who are committed enough to want to keep on top of the fixtures, making their transfers during each short, closely spaced game week, organise their bench and keep an eye out for players who are being rotated and as a result won't get as much game time. It is a full-time job during the festive break. Yes, Mum's busy cooking Christmas dinner. Yes, Dad's making sure everyone's got drinks. Yes, nephews and nieces are running around off their face on chocolate coins. That's *their* jobs. Fantasy football is yours.

You will have mates who can't keep on top of it. They may know that game week 19 runs between 22 and 24 December, sure, but do they know that game week 20 begins on Boxing Day and only lasts until 27 December?

Not to mention game week 21, which slides so covertly down their chimney on 28 December that they don't even realise, and, *poof*, it's gone in a puff of tinsel the next evening. Add a final, hungover game week 22 that rolls around stinking of eggnog on New Year's Day, and the next thing the unprepared fantasy football manager knows is that he's 55 points behind everyone else in his mini-league wondering where the time went. The time went on game weeks 20, 21 and 22, when you were busy eating, drinking and sleeping.

If you have a planner, spreadsheet or diary to help you navigate the absolute minefield of the Christmas fixtures, then you probably want to ask Santa to put some friends and/or a social life in your stocking next year, but, hey, we're not here to judge. You'll be benefitting from using your weekly transfers, rotating your bench, changing your captain accordingly, while certain other individuals who don't have a colour-coded wall chart are probably out at festive parties, drinking and getting off with people. Losers.

There's a fine line between letting the stresses of fantasy football management ruin your Christmas and doing so little that you drop even further behind that mate in your mini-league whose team is already worth £1.4m more than yours and owns six different coloured highlighters. Maybe make a little note somewhere. Maybe set a few alarms on your phone. Maybe when your Aunty Sandra asks what you want for Christmas, you tell her that you need someone to remind you when you're in between game weeks so you can keep an eye on the players that Man City are rotating, in the hope you can scrape together a starting 11 likely to get some actual minutes between them. But, let's be honest, it'll be socks from Sandra. It's always fucking socks from Sandra.

Anyone would be forgiven for overlooking one of the windows between game weeks during the Christmas fixtures, they're as small and easily unnoticeable as Darius Vassell in an England shirt. But some cock-ups and misfortunes are bigger. Much bigger. Like Peter Crouch on Andy Carroll's shoulders with a long coat on, pretending to be one person to gain access to the 'World Class Premier League Striker Hall of Fame'. That's how big some tales of woe are. So gargantuan that over the seasons they become more than mere tales of unbelievable hardship, bad luck and stupidity, they gain a status that elevates them to folklore, to legend.

Urban legends have existed for centuries. We've all heard apocryphal tales in our lifetimes – shouted in playgrounds or whispered in pubs – like the one about the axe-wielding maniac who realised he had been caught masturbating by his mum because she'd left a hot cup of tea next to his bed, or the boy who couldn't hear someone banging his dad's head on the top of the car because he had his headphones on. Some of them may be remembered incorrectly and passed down through generations, changing and evolving through each incorrect telling. Some were clearly horseshit to begin with and could never have occurred, regardless of how many times it has been told over the years. For instance, I don't know who it was who managed to witness the man who jumped to his death from a skyscraper at 5pm exactly, after he was told he'd get a phone call at five if his business hadn't gone bust – only to hear his phone ringing as he hurtled past the window of his own office. Yes, there was the bloke that put peanut butter on his nether regions and got his dog to lick it off in his living room when his entire family jumped out from behind his furniture to surprise him for his birthday. Yes, there was the bloke who went to hospital with a bottle of tomato ketchup up his bottom and gave an elaborate story about locking himself out of his house and falling on to the sauce when he was attempting to shimmy up the drainpipe, only for the doctor to remove the sauce and find a condom attached.

As well as these stalwarts of childhood, every country, industry or, in our case, pastime, have their own urban legends. As a chubby child, I was an avid fan of fast food and there were a hell of a lot of horror stories linked to my favourite pastime that were doing the rounds, and every single one of them scared the bejesus out of me. There was the tale of the girl who asked for a chicken sandwich without any mayonnaise in a popular fast food establishment, only to find that when she bit into the sandwich an excess of mayonnaise exploded over her face. She rightfully took the sandwich back to the counter to complain, where she was told by staff that it wasn't mayonnaise and she had, instead, bitten into a chicken's ulcer. Now, I can't imagine that the employees at that particular fast food chain would have performed a post-mortem on the sandwich that quickly, there and then at the counter, regardless of how many stars they had on their name badge. Plus, I also very much doubt they would have corrected the girl – who was simply asking for a replacement chicken sandwich, just without the mayonnaise this time – that she had in fact bitten into an ulcer and that she actually had chicken pus all over her face. Just a thought. But as a tubby youngster, I didn't question all the issues and plot holes in the narrative, I just worried that one day I too would get a mouthful of hot, thick, white fowl discharge – almost enough to put you off eating fast food completely … *almost* enough; nothing actually stopped me eating fast food as a kid, I just used to have to eat it really quickly with my eyes closed like a dog, so that if I did get an unwanted mouthful, I wouldn't know about it. God, where were my parents?

Fantasy football urban legends are particularly interesting and, despite what you might think after reading a couple of paragraphs about poultry ulcers, more in keeping with the overall tone of the book. Of course, there's the famous tale of the fantasy Premier League player who triple captained Gastón Ramírez the week he got -2 points. Treble that to -6. Yep. Why someone would feel the compulsion to use their triple captain chip, the once-a-season lifeline, the single nuclear weapon that can change your fortunes and help you destroy your enemies, on then-Middlesbrough attacking-midfielder Gastón Ramírez is beyond me. I mean, there's picking a differential, then there's just being a silly sausage. The validity of this particular nugget of bad luck – or, more accurately – bad *judgement* has been corroborated to a certain extent as thousands will have seen the infamous moment, captured forever as a screenshot. While there are a lot of photoshoppers out there forging just these types of scenarios in attempts to go viral, I believe that the fable of the triple captaining of Ramírez on the game week he got sent off is gospel.

There was the tale of the staunch Chelsea hater who wrestled with his conscience for weeks before biting the bullet and putting Willian in his team, only for Willian's mum to sadly and suddenly pass away only a couple of hours later, forcing the Brazilian out of the Chelsea squad for a couple of weeks. This particular gentleman tweeted us his news, pointing out the irony and adding '#Voodoo' for good measure.

You hear a myriad of horror stories on a weekly basis if you keep up with the right hashtags and threads, so we trawled through the annals of fantasy football social media, where hatred, loathing and regret reign supreme. You can find accounts of fantasy football heartache relating to nearly every scenario and every player in every team, although it's proven more difficult to find the managers willing to admit that they transferred in Adam Johnson the week before he was released from his contract with Sunderland for, well, you know. Schoolgirl error.

Some moan about getting rid of Sergio Agüero that fateful week he netted five, some about bringing in Sadio Mané and putting the captain's armband on him the week he was sent off for kicking Ederson in the face. There are grumbles from those who never picked Riyad Mahrez or Jamie Vardy the year Leicester won the Premier League title because they had to stop scoring eventually, right? Then there's equally pained cries from those who did bring them in, but did it the following season instead, and we all know how that went. On the subject of Riyad Mahrez and his fantastic 2015/16 season, one anonymous Reddit user documents that he decided to bring the winger in after he scored an impressive brace against Everton, only for him to then not score or even provide a single assist for the next five weeks and even miss two penalties! The pissed-off manager eventually transferred him out and, of course, he instantly began returning big points again, finding the form that helped Leicester to win the title.

One unlucky individual on a forum admits to buying Paul Pogba a mere three minutes before he received a red card and the subsequent ban that goes with it. This tragic chap was forced to instantly take the mandatory four-point penalty to replace him and did so for Aaron Ramsey, who went on to get a single point before getting injured for three weeks. It never rains but it pours.

It's these niggly little things that, on the face of it, shouldn't bother you at all; things that a non-fantasy football player (a *fuggle*, if you will) would shrug at. Your other half probably won't understand why the seemingly insignificant inconvenience of taking out Alexis Sanchez the week he scored a hat-trick has put you in a bad mood for the entirety of the weekend, but there are no trivial tales of woe here; every story is *Sophie's Choice* when it happens to you.

Running a large fantasy football podcast and social media account for the last five years means that we have seen our fair share of the aforementioned woe. To be honest, when you've played fantasy football as long as we have you probably have enough of *your own* anecdotes to fill a book, but that would be self-indulgent, and if there's one thing that the award-winning Gaffer Tapes is not, it's self-indulgent. We literally said that to our mate, *Lord of the Rings* actor Dominic Monaghan, the other day over really, *really* expensive cocktails. But a game week won't go by where someone doesn't tell us a horror story. Sometimes it's their own fault and they hold their hands up and take ownership of the mistake. Sometimes, on the other hand, there is an external force at play and they ask us to share their story with sympathetic, like-minded individuals who will understand their pain, and, of course, rip the piss out of them mercilessly on social media for likes and retweets.

To thousands and thousands of people, The Gaffer Tapes have been like a fantasy football 'Dear Deidre' (good name for a new feature: write that down) and we would be remiss if we didn't mention just a few of these day-to-day tales of woe and fantasy football niggles (let's call them *figgles*).

In the true spirit of community and fair play, we should start by talking about a few of our own stories of grief that have emerged whilst playing the game. Even if you've only played one single season of fantasy football, you will have at least one story that would qualify for some column inches here, so how could we discuss accounts of hardship without spilling our own beans all over the pages.

Our very own Craig Hazell once made a bleary eyed, pre-caffeinated transfer on a Saturday morning and took out the wrong player. It was part of a masterplan he had been cooking up for a week, and it was step one of a pair of well thought-out transfers. A waning Harry Kane and Danny Ings were to make way for Pierre Emerick Aubameyang and Callum Wilson, who had both hit colossal form and were staring at a run of tantalising upcoming fixtures. Saturday morning rolls around, as it tends to do – more often than not following a Friday night – and our hero logs into his fantasy football team, rubbing the sleep from his eyes. He knows what he has to do, he's known for a while, and this, the actual, physical execution of the plan, is the easy bit. Working out which strategy you're going to use and deciding to stick with it is the hard bit – the rest is plain sailing. Remembering your password and being able to read the players' names is surely the very simplest aspect of the weekly transfer, right? Not if you're award-winning Craig Hazell.

Sergio Agüero taken out and Aubameyang brought in. Confirm button pressed; stage one complete. No going back. This is great fun. Life is good. Now, to get rid of the incompetent Danny Ings who has been nothing but an unwelcome stain on this beautiful team for a month now. Ings taken out, Callum Wilson selected … but hang on. What? Insufficient funds to buy Wilson? But the money had been worked out beforehand and there was plenty. This must be a glitch. The money from Kane and Ings was more than enough to buy Aubameyang and Wilson. The game is faulty, there will be a lawsuit damn it! Social media will be all over this. There will be interviews with Philip and Holly on *This Morning*, Martin Glenn, head of the Football Association will write a formal apology, even Prince William, in his official capacity as president of the FA, will be grovelling for forgiveness after this clear and blatant mathematical error on behalf of the official fantasy Premier League game. Oh shit, he took out the wrong player. The penny, or rather, *several million* pennies, suddenly dropped. Craig had removed Sergio Agüero, in the form of his career and playing with a City side that's been hailed as one of the very best to ever grace the game, may I add, instead of the more expensive, underscoring, certainly not value for money Harry Kane. Now, there are insufficient funds for Callum Wilson. In a scene reminiscent of the Tom Hanks movie *Castaway*, please picture our tragic hero clawing at his laptop, crying, screaming 'Wilson!' over and over again, knowing that he was gone forever. 'I'm sorry Wilson!' The compromise was to pick up a cheaper option in Kelechi Iheanacho, who of course got the obligatory two points. Of course, Harry Kane does the same and blanks. Of course, Callum Wilson scores a brace, and finally, the ultimate kick in the volleyball, *OF COURSE* Sergio Agüero scores and gets an assist too. The only way it could have gone worse for Craig on that day was if he'd been shot by a Nazi like Tom Hanks in *Saving Private Ryan*, taken hostage by Somali pirates like Tom Hanks in *Captain Phillips*, or contracted full-blown Aids like Tom Hanks when he ate too much *Philadelphia*.

The blame for that story couldn't be passed on to anyone else. Craig took responsibility for his own glaring mistake and as a result refuses to even log in to his fantasy football team before having several strong espressos and a line of speed to keep him alert and focussed. However, Craig was victim of another fable of despair in which he did absolutely nothing wrong other than showing too much trust in his fellow man. After The Gaffer Tapes performed a live show in a sold-out venue in London's West End, we left the cheering audience and walked off stage feeling like kings as the praise and adulation reverberated around the theatre, an hour of top-quality entertainment had well and truly been enjoyed by everyone in attendance. Unfortunately, the euphoria was to be short lived, as an unsuspecting Craig Hazell had not only left his laptop on the stage, but he was logged in to his fantasy football team. A moment's silence please.

This scenario is one of the many holy grails for fantasy football players around the globe. A mate leaves his laptop or phone unattended for any length of time and his team is wide open to sabotage, as was the case on this fateful occasion. Back in the day if a mate left his phone on the table at the pub and went for a piss before those phones had internet access – yes, there was a time – then the mandatory procedure was to text the immortal phrase 'I love cock' to as many people in their phonebook as possible before they got back. I think one of my mates managed 23 on mine. It was the reply of 'I always wondered, son' from my mum that really hurt though.

Not content with receiving a five-star comedy fantasy football show, complete with interactive quiz and prizes, an unspecified number of assailants – whose identities are still unknown to The Gaffer Tapes at the time this book went to print – did maliciously and with callous disregard fiddle with another manager's team. An unwanted fantasy football fiddle (or *faddle*) is a very serious crime. Technically, there's no current penalty for it, but if the particular faddle in question costs significant points then surely the punishment should be equally significant. I'm not saying we need to bring back public flogging, but what about private flogging? Fantasy football flogging (you know where we're going with this) would be a decent deterrent. If people knew that you would get a merciless and thorough *fagging* then maybe it would make them think twice before violating the sanctity of another manager's team. That's their baby, their beautifully tuned, perfected brainchild that has been sullied by someone having a laugh. Well, you know who isn't laughing? Someone who's being privately fagged in a dark room, that's who. It transpired that the unwanted transfer that was forced upon Craig's team was the removal of Sergio Agüero, who at the time, as he nearly always is, was firing on all cylinders, in favour of Watford's Jerome Sinclair. Craig left Sinclair in his team in the hope that poetic justice would take force and he would have an amazing anecdote of moral victory. Alas, Sinclair played 12 minutes, got booked and confirmed Craig's belief in atheism.

In all honesty, the faddle could have been more excessive, with several top players being removed and replaced with an entire team of guys who never see a minute of football, costing a fortune in points hits too. We assume that the saboteur/saboteurs were startled by something, maybe a passing soundman or falling light rig, and they scuttled off back into the shadows, but while Craig was particularly unhappy about being violated in this way, he understood in hindsight that it could have been a lot worse. They could have shared his internet history with the entire audience.

But it can't just be Craig's team that receives the scrutiny and ridicule, although it is fun, the other two have had their fair share of horror stories when it comes to 'the game of the beautiful game'.

There are over 400 footballers in the Premier League, and as a result a hell of a lot of players to choose from for your fantasy football team. Some of these players tend to have the same surname, which can be confusing. I mean, not to them it's not, but to the average person it might be, right? Right, guys? There might be a couple of Smiths, Joneses, Silvas, Davises. But when the surname is not only a little more unique, but there are two players with that same unique surname playing in *the same team*, then, let's be completely honest, you are taking the mick, mate.

Yes, Tom Holmes transferred in the wrong Ayew brother. Was it a lack of concentration? Complacency? Contemplation? Comtemplacency? Who knows? Tom wanted the in-form, much talked about André Ayew, who had been playing brilliantly on the wing for Swansea for weeks, racking up great points despite his tricky fixtures. Now, with a nice run of very winnable games ahead of him and an incredibly low price-tag and percentage ownership, he would be an absolutely genius acquisition. Tom would look like the fantasy football guru he had always believed himself to be … despite actually hearing about how good André Ayew was from a fella down the boozer. However, Tom *didn't* want *Jordan* Ayew, who wasn't getting a game and didn't have all the other good, genius stuff that was just mentioned. Obviously, this being a tale of woe, Jordan goes in, the confirm button is pressed and Tom curses Mrs Ayew for encouraging both her sons to become footballers when one of them would be just as happy being a stand-up comedian, who could have called his debut arena tour 'Ayew Having a Laugh?' I bet she feels stupid now.

The realisation didn't come instantly for Tom, as he assumed he had correctly transferred in André. There was even a small fist pump and celebratory jig when André got a last-minute assist and was sure to be on for a bonus point or two. Genius status had been applied for and the fantasy football gods were reviewing the very valid application. But hold on. Once the final whistle had gone in the last of the 3pm kick-offs and it was time to have a cheeky look at the scores on the doors so far, *Ayew Having a Laugh* was the right sentiment indeed. What had happened? How had André got zero points? Nothing? Not a sausage? He'd played the full 90 minutes, got an assist and a clean sheet. That was six points just there! But a click on the player's profile revealed the true horror of the situation. Jordan didn't play, Jordan didn't get a single point, Jordan let us all down, he really should have taken up comedy.

The pain was only marginally lessened by the fact that Tom was able to repeatedly use the phrase 'Ayew two brothers?' whenever he told the anecdote for the following fortnight, but eventually that novelty wore off and all that was left was an empty void that could only have been filled by six lovely points. The fact that Tom was eventually beaten in his office mini-league that season by just four points only rubbed further salt into the wound. To this day, Tom can't read an article about Peter *Andre* or Katie Price aka *Jordan* without becoming instantly furious. Not because of the Ayew brothers case of mistaken identity, but because he can't stand Peter Andre and Jordan. They're absolute cretins.

Ash Kernsworth, however, a man who finished 81st in the whole world at fantasy football in the 2011/12 season and 850th overall in 2017/18 out of nearly six million people, has surely never made a glaring error, or hides his own fable of utter stupidity … Ash decided, on a stag-do in Amsterdam, to use his wildcard. At three o'clock in the morning. Drunk. Yeah, that probably falls under the 'fable of utter stupidity' category, or if not it has to be filed next to it in the 'is he *actually* ill?' section.

There's something in us that decides doing stupid things is actually a good idea when we're drunk. In fact, it's worse than that. There's often something screaming at you that it is absolutely the MOST IMPORTANT THING IN THE WORLD that you do said stupid thing and you won't be able to be happy again until you've done it. Climbing a tree on your way home from the pub is a good example. You've never been a tree climber, not even as a child when it is a lot more socially acceptable to do so. You've never contemplated climbing a tree, but as the midnight hour strikes and you're stumbling home, several lemonades to the wind, in autopilot, you suddenly notice that tree you pass nearly every day. Tonight, it is your Everest. Sober, you would probably say something along the lines of 'that's pointless and dangerous, how about you *don't* climb the tree and get yourself home to bed because you have to be up for work in six hours'. But sober you isn't here tonight. Sober you got his coat and left at about half past eight that evening when Gary suggested having 'just one more' for the third time. Sober you doesn't know of the tree, of the quest, of destiny. Let's be honest, sober you is a bit of a boffin.

The ascent of the tree, or perhaps the stealing of the traffic cone, riding of the shopping trolley, dancing on the bus stop roof, never looks as aesthetically pleasing as you imagine in your booze-addled mind, but then it doesn't matter because you've completed your mission. You feel sated, satisfied, complete and, other than a potentially sprained ankle, a cracked rib and a *tiny* bit of a traffic cone going up your bottom, you've made it out the other side relatively unscathed. The next morning, it will be a vague, hazy memory. For Ash 'the wildcard of Amsterdam' Kernsworth, the next morning he was not unscathed, he could not simply shrug off a vague memory, a coat full of leaves and a sore bottom and move on. Damage had been done. Irreparable damage.

After a lethal cocktail of cherry beer, normal beer and more cherry beer, Ash decided that, rather than go to sleep in the nice, warm, comfortable hotel bed, he would start running up his data roaming costs and have a little look at his team. Why not? It was a Friday night/Saturday morning, the transfer deadline was in a mere eight and a half hours, and he would be remiss as a legitimate fantasy football expert if he didn't weigh up his options and decide on his weekly moves. The problem with having a drunken 3am tinker is that you can often lose control and take it too far. Cherry beer-driven inhibition took over and a little tinker became a larger tinker, the larger tinker became a significant tinker and the significant tinker became an *activate wildcard* tinker. Players were transferred in who would never have usually seen the light of day in the fantasy football team of someone who is genuinely good at the game. Hunches were followed through with, guesswork was confirmed with gusto, whims were executed, never to be looked back upon. Drunk Ash was in his element. Drunk Ash was loving life.

Sober Ash, however … not so much. Sober Ash didn't do things like this. Sober Ash wouldn't normally take a point hit to transfer in a second player, let alone go to the lengths he did to change his entire squad. But most unfortunate of all, Sober Ash didn't wake up until 12:30pm.

He didn't remember the tinkering. There was no recollection of being so footloose and fancy free. This sombre, slightly dehydrated Ash didn't realise what damage he had done whilst under the influence of copious amounts of the sweet, red, Dutch nectar. He simply drank some water, smashed down a couple of painkillers and a Berocca and went out to fulfil his touristic needs by viewing some of the glorious sights and sounds of Amsterdam. It wasn't until the subject of the football scores came up a little later that something, some vague memory, began to surface at the back of Ash's mind. A faint recollection, almost like a dream, was working its way to the forefront of his consciousness; it was hazy at first, but the more the conversation about that day's games continued to resonate around him, the more the fog began to clear, until … oh god, no! NO!

As he grabbed for his phone, the realisation, the memories, began to flood back like when you are reminded of a particularly vague nightmare or worrying erotic dream about a work colleague that you can't stand. Figures began appearing in Ash's mind as he attempted to log in. Tom Ince appeared before vanishing in a puff of smoke. Surely not. A dark, hooded figure loomed, before disappearing. Why was it taking so long to log in? Jermaine Jenas? No, he was a pundit now, wasn't he? Surely he hadn't picked a fucking pundit! Maybe it was Jermain Defoe he'd put in his team. Oh god, maybe it was both! The mysterious, hooded man appeared once again. Who was he? What had Drunk Ash done? Damn you cherry beer, what had you made Drunk Ash do?! But all was soon revealed.

The carefully thought-out team that had been sitting in a respectable position somewhere within the top 1 per cent was no more. Gone. In their wake was a group of misfits, renegades and nobodies who were more akin to the Home Guard from *Dad's Army* than a dream team – quite literally, some of them were incredibly old. Ash winced as he scanned the team he had drunkenly selected. Why? What had possessed him? That player didn't play anymore. That one wasn't *the worst* player in the world, but he's playing for *them* so he was averaging two points a week. *That bloke* couldn't hit a cow's arse *or* a barn door with several banjos and … oh no, it can't be. The dark figure that had been looming on the fringes of his consciousness stepped forward slowly and began to remove his cloak as Ash gazed upon the final names on the screen in front of him. He couldn't have, surely. What had possessed him? Finally, realisation hit as the full team came into view and the hooded man finally revealed his face … it had been Andy Carroll all along. Well, Scooby-Doo could get fucked, because there was no way Ash was going to get away with it, not after all those pesky cherry beers.

Over the next few hours, as Ash sat in a bar watching goal after goal go in from players who he had previously owned and got rid of, and bench after bench being warmed by the ones he had replaced them with, he tried to understand what his drunken rationale had been. The booze had made him too confident, too wild. He'd been picturing glory, trying to foresee that random Peter Crouch hat-trick, the last-minute John O'Shea winner and the fourth-choice Burnley striker's out-of-the-blue brace against Man United, because things like that *did* occur now and then, and if they happened in the next few weeks Ash would look like the greatest fantasy football manager on Earth. Granted, it was a tad more difficult to see the thought behind some of the other choices, not to mention the fact that as a result of being able to rename your team on a wildcard Ash had to see out the rest of the season as the proud manager of 'The Cherrrrrry Boyyyz LOL'.

It's safe to say that cherry beer gate didn't occur in one of the seasons when Ash finished in the top 100, and it is an indelible blotch on his otherwise pristine record. A blotch that acts as a constant, permanent reminder not to climb that tree when you're drunk.

The Boot Room

WHAT is the boot room? Apart from being a feature we attempted once on our podcast, which died on its arse because we hadn't planned it and ended up just shouting at each other for ten minutes and not actually knowing why, the boot room is a Pandora's box of evils. The boot room is also a cathartic process of cleansing, a way of ranting about things you despise. The boot room is a room where we 'boot out' and banish things we hate from fantasy football, forever. But most importantly, I am legally obliged to inform you that the boot room is first and foremost absolutely nothing like the long-standing British television show *Room 101*, where people banish things they don't like to a room, forever. I simply cannot stress that enough.

Sure, we all want to throw in the fantasy football staples of the player who gets injured 35 seconds after you bring him in and the bloke who gets minus points the one time you captain him. Of course, we want to exile the guy that is on for a clean sheet and then scores a spectacular 88th-minute own goal, or the fella you thought hard about picking but didn't, who predictably then scores a hat-trick. But these are what makes the game of fantasy football so good, so intriguing, so unmissable, so bloody unique. We couldn't banish these little annoyances and eccentricities, it would be like *The X Factor* without Simon Cowell, or *Match of the Day* without Mark Lawrenson; yeah, it's annoying (*incredibly-so* in the case of the latter), but it's all part of it. It wouldn't be the same without them.

The below list of elements that we would like to kick right into the boot room and out of fantasy football for eternity are very different. The game wouldn't miss them; in fact, the game would be much better without them and their malevolence.

Wildcard

For those of you who were bought this book by a grandparent who had absolutely no idea what your real interests were but knew you liked football when you were seven, then a wildcard is an opportunity to change your entire squad without suffering any point loss. At least you will know this for next year when they inevitably buy you the same gift. Age is a cruel mistress. The rest of you will no doubt be questioning our credentials as your wildcard has saved your season on many occasions. Elsewhere in this book we have also described it as the most useful tool in beating your mates, and it is. There's no doubting that a well-timed wildcard can be the catalyst you need to rise up your league, but at what cost to your mental state? At the best of times, fantasy football can take over your Saturday morning. You can subconsciously agree to lunch with the in-laws and a *Pitch Perfect* movie marathon while you're making those final changes to your line-up. Joke's on her, by the way, I love *Pitch Perfect*. A wildcard, though, consumes your whole week. If you make your decision early, and you should, then you will hit that WC button on a Sunday night. Worse still, you might do it on an international break to give yourself a full two weeks. That's a full fortnight of tinkering. That's enough fiddling to make yourself blind. Every transfer you make is another potential regret that will haunt you on the final weekend of the season. All those players you didn't have the chance to be envious of because you could never afford them are now yours to have. It's like looking at the menu in a TGI Fridays. There's far too much choice, all of them will make you hate yourself afterwards and why are all of them covered in Jack Daniel's sauce? Not only that, but there's so much expectation that goes with it. Your mates will ask you 'have you wilcarded?' and then all of a sudden anything less than 80 points is an absolute disaster. Seven days of painstaking back and forth and agonising decisions only to get the same shitty results you would've got without it. You got through every position in your squad, narrowing it down to a couple of possible players, and each one is like *Sophie's Choice* except both kids are little bastards you don't think you want anyway. The whole process is exhausting and one you wish you could avoid altogether. Unless, that is, you get it absolutely bang on. In those cases, we bloody love wildcards. You'd be mad not to.

Friday night kick-offs

Friday nights mean different things to different people. If you're in your 40s, for instance, it might mean Chris Evans, Ocean Colour Scene and iconic rock 'n' roll television. If you're in your 30s it could mean Alan Carr, Justin Lee Collins and catchphrase comedy sketches. Or if you're Justin Lee Collins's wife it might mean another night of journaling your sexual thoughts and learning to sleep with your eyes open. Whoever you are, though, there's one thing that definitely isn't synonymous with Friday nights and that's football. There was a time when all matches were played at 3pm on a Saturday and football occupied such a small portion of the weekend. You can probably learn about it in books or by asking your grandad about Bovril and waiting half an hour until he finally gets to it. Be warned, though, that conversation will likely end up in a rant about footballers who wear gloves and immigration. Thankfully, those days are gone and every weekend we are treated to a televisual smorgasbord of games. You can be drinking your coffee on a Saturday morning, explaining to Eden Hazard why you're not captaining him this week, and before you know it it's 8pm and you're still in your boxer shorts having feasted on back-to-back-to-back matches. You're also now possibly single. That's football. We've all made peace with the sacrifices we have to make in order to follow the game we love and where fantasy football fits into that weekly schedule. Then some genius, who is definitely single, decided that they could extend football viewing to Friday night. On a European week, that's seven consecutive days of football, and I don't mean that in a good way. What kind of messed up fantasy football deadline is 6.30pm on a Friday?! It's as if they didn't even think of Ryan from the HSBC in Andover and his hilariously named Exeter Gently when they put together this multi-billion-pound TV deal. At a time when you are likely travelling home, making dinner for the kids or, worse still, staying late in the office, you should be in your virtual safe space picking 11 gladiators to take you into a weekend of battle. Thanks a lot Premier League; now my children are crying because they're hungry! One missed deadline on a Friday night could completely ruin your fantasy weekend and all because someone, somewhere, thought we'd want to watch Cardiff vs Brighton instead of *Gogglebox*. One thing's for sure, I won't be allowing any unemployed people in my league next year. You don't get 73 quid a week AND a distinct advantage in the mini-league. It's one or the other mate! Get a job or get a new hobby!

The Europa League

Thursdays are alright, aren't they? Arguably the fourth-best day of the week after Friday and the weekend. 'Thirsty Thursday' seems to be a new craze, where, get this, people drink alcohol on a Thursday night and post pictures of themselves and/or the drinks they are currently drinking on social media, accompanied by the phrase 'Thirsty Thursday'. Crazy bastards. Little tip for you, though, alcohol dehydrates you, and if you truly *are* thirsty on a Thursday, or any other day of the week come to that, your best option is to consume water or perhaps some kind of sports drink. Not only is this good advice, but also what I reply to the pictures of individuals attempting to quench their thirst with large glasses of white wine. You're doing it all wrong! God, I'm good fun on social media.

Thursdays can also be a day of ridicule. Coming fifth in the Premier League table at the end of the season is no mean feat. The Prem is arguably the best league in the world, and by finishing fifth, or even sixth, it means that you have done better than a lot of teams, filled with a lot of expensive players. It should be seen as an achievement. Yeah, you didn't make it into the Champions League with Europe's elite, and instead you are stuck with the ugly and less successful cousin, but you're still playing European football.

As soon as a team misses out on those top-four places and is guaranteed qualification into the Europa League for next season, the jokes begin. 'Let's hope Arsenal fans clear their diaries for Thursdays next year.' 'I bet Chelsea fans are gutted they'll be missing *The One Show* on a Thursday.' It's an absolute staple of football-based mockery. There was also a period when it was derogatorily referred to as 'The Channel 5 Cup', which we all know is the ultimate slur.

Thursdays suddenly becoming busier than usual isn't the reason why we are selecting the Europa League to go and jump head first into the boot room. It is, in fact, because it's just a bit shit. Not only is it just a bit shit, but it can actually have negative fantasy football ramifications. If a player in your fantasy side gets injured in a Champions League game against one of the giants of European football like Juventus, Barcelona or PSG, then, as annoying as it is, it is kind of justified because of the magnitude of the game. Maybe he doesn't get injured, but instead he's rested in the weekend's Premier League fixture you were hoping he would play in so that he'll be fit for the Champions League clash with the bigger boys midweek. Again, annoying, yet understandable. But for one of your players, one of the 15 men you have put faith in by selecting them for your carefully thought-out squad, to miss a game through injury or rotation because of the *Europa fucking League?!* I am missing out on getting a single minute for my player because of your Thursday game against someone like AEK Larnaca, København, FC Krasnodar or AC Milan?! Ridiculous. How can that mickey mouse cup take precedence over Burnley away on Sunday? Come on. So now, Mr Thursday Night Manager, I'm not only getting zero points for the guy *you* decided to play in the Europa-bastard-League, but he's going to be replaced by a player off my bench who is crap and will get two points if I'm lucky. Yes, I said a second ago that my squad was made up of 15 carefully thought-out men, but, let's be honest, it's 11 carefully thought-out men and four cheap knobheads. And cheap knobhead number one will be making a cameo at the weekend because of you, and the Europa bloody League.

The January transfer window

The winter transfer window was met with harsh criticism when it was introduced in 2003/04, with lower league managers even claiming it could drive clubs out of business. I was annoyed mainly because the thought of not being able to sign a player whenever I wanted on Football Manager ruined the whole experience for me and put me off playing it for a while. If only it had been introduced earlier, it might have had as equal an impact on my virginity as it did on world football. Since then, it has become an accepted annual occurrence and there's a generation of fans who, as well as seeing Gary Lineker as a TV presenter and Pele as the bloke off the erection adverts, do not know any different, but my relationship with it has always been fraught.

The summer transfer window is something you can reason with. A club might make 11 new signings, all for the first team, but you can check out their line-ups in friendlies, you can see who they've sold and where their weaknesses are. The January window, on the other hand, is a toddler. There's no rationalising with it. Liverpool want a striker? No problem, here's Andy Carroll. He's injury prone, looks equine and shares a flat with Kevin Nolan because he can't be trusted on his own. That'll be £35m, please. The pressure of a winter move can be enough to turn the most in-form striker into a shivering wreck. Just ask Fernando Torres. And it all has a knock-on effect on your fantasy football team. On the one hand, you have the incoming players. They're new, they're shiny, they're exciting and when you hear all the hype from Jim White and his dazzling yellow tie it's really hard not to be utterly convinced he will score 73 goals by March. It's never been done before in the history of the game, but that YouTube compilation they keep showing is *really* good. Plus, they've priced him up at an ambiguous £8m, which could fit in nicely. The reason they're doing this, by the way, is because they also have absolutely no idea how good he is going to be. Every ounce of logic in you tells you to avoid this new kid in school at all costs, but you can't help looking at him like Little Mo did at Trevor in Eastenders, convincing yourself he will be different this time.

There's also another downside to this month-long headache. You might have your third striker slot all sewn up with a guy who has solidly knocked in seven or eight goals by Christmas and is so cheap he allows you to have a star-studded midfield. He's perfect. Then Bournemouth go out and spend 20 million quid and you know they don't spend that kind of money willy-nilly. Unless it's on a two-bed detached cottage – property is extortionate down there. Even though your guy has done great, they've had a sniff of top-half football and all of a sudden blown all this money on Rodrigo Goal-Machine, who could completely blow up your squad. Worse still, you have those huge marquee signings in January like Aubameyang or Van Dijk that you just know you have to be a part of. You see those picked percentages on the up every day and just know it's a bandwagon you have to jump on, only for him to be eased in gently and leave you with one point for his 12-minute cameo in a 4-0 win. It's a nightmare and enough to give you seasonally affected disorder.

Managers

First things first, I don't hate managers. I have friends who are managers, how can I? I actually feel sorry for them, and it's the absurdity of the nature of their job that leads to them becoming one of the most frustrating aspects of fantasy football. A change of manager can throw your line-up into chaos and given the high-pressure nature of their job, it happens a lot. The team who came up via the play-offs can be sat in 20th place in October and their manager will find themselves job hunting. Of course they're 20th! They're officially the 20th-best team in the league before a ball is kicked! They're on target! The team in last place losing their manager might not immediately affect you, obviously. You're not likely to have three players from the worst team in the league, and if you do then this isn't the chapter you should be reading right now. The sacked manager syndrome is very real though, and if Huddersfield relieve their gaffer of his duties the week before you were set to captain your in-form striker against them, it can be a real bastard. For whatever reason, an awful team can find themselves galvanised under a new boss, or even without one, and what was a banker of ten points suddenly becomes a washout. You only need to look at Ole Gunnar Solskjær's impact at Old Trafford to see what turns an impotent group of zero pointers into fantasy football necessities.

That's not to say a new manager always brings good fortune, and a change at the helm can stitch you right up if you own his players. You might have Mr Reliable in midfield who has played 38 out of 38 games for five seasons without picking up a single booking. He's club captain, all-round good guy, and they're halfway through his bronze statue outside the ground. All of a sudden Alan Pardew has somehow hypnotised a chairman into giving him a job again, he's dropped Mr Reliable on his first day and turned the statue into a centaur. That's the other thing about managers, they have complete autonomy over their team selection, and therefore yours. One man can completely ruin your game week. It's a lot of trust to put in the hands of a single individual, and for whatever reason we always give them the benefit of the doubt that they might actually know what they're doing. On the whole, football managers are just ex-footballers. Those same footballers we mercilessly mock for being idiots and turn into memes for their moments of irrational stupidity. Then they retire, turn 40 and pop on a suit, and all of a sudden we are asking them questions about Brexit. They're the same people who said pacifically instead of specifically and insist they 'bought' their own ideas with them. Why are we all of a sudden giving them so much kudos? Let's not forget Manchester City once let Stuart Pearce, a man who put David James up front, unironically, oversee their empire. They're not to be trusted!

Auto-pick

If you profess to be a real fantasy football player then these two hyphenated words might mean absolutely nothing to you. If they do, then I hope you agree in saying that a lucky dip is for fairgrounds and lottery tickets. For those of you who don't know, the auto-pick feature magically picks your squad, keeping you within budget and legal formations. It's a feature that we really have outgrown and evolved beyond, but for some reason it still exists. It's the appendix of the fantasy football world. Granted, this isn't a compelling reason to have so much vitriol towards it that you'd want to banish it into a fictional boot room forever, but if you imagine losing out to these cowboys who let a computer pick their team then you might start to understand the disdain.

Back in the newspaper days of the game, my mum would humour me by feigning interest in fantasy football, and she reluctantly agreed to join my league with my dad. She knew absolutely nothing about football, which was exactly why I invited her. I wanted another couple of quid in the kitty and the reassurance that I wouldn't finish last. Yes, I was an extremely manipulative ten-year-old, but that's not the story. All of the players had serial numbers and she would simply reel off 11 numbers and that would make up her side. It was usually an absolute shit show of selections. Substitute goalkeepers, youth players, defensive midfielders, fat children with asthma, foreign kids who spouted racial stereotypes, girls who weren't allowed to join the team, you know all the usuals. However, there was one year that she managed to get herself Cantona and Fowler up front just by shouting weird binary at me and ended up winning. That was that. The random picking was shit and I wouldn't tolerate it any longer. In the age of the internet, though, where we no longer need our mums to make up the numbers at our party, there really is no excuse for handing over your team selection to Lady Luck. That first squad pick can be absolute agony, lying in a pool of sweat surrounded by scraps of paper, a chewed-up pencil and an abacus. It's a rite of passage that we should all have to endure. There will be some of your friends who claim they use it just to give them a canvas to work with. They will keep hitting the button until it throws up a half-good combination and work from there. It's up to you, but I wouldn't tolerate it. All it takes for evil to triumph is for good men to do nothing.

Football social media

Back in the day, footballers would keep themselves to themselves. Now, I'm not saying they were saints. In fact, it is quite the opposite – they were up to all sorts – but it was just that not everyone was aware of it back then. In 2014 I compered an event in which former Bristol City and Bristol Rovers players did some after-dinner speaking. I won't mention their names, not because I want to keep them anonymous, but because I genuinely can't remember what their names were. Their footballing careers took place in the 70s and, I'll hold my hands up, my knowledge of Second and Third Division players from the decade before I was born is relatively shoddy. Apart from it being one of the weirdest experiences of my life and probably the easiest money I've ever made, it dawned on me that evening just how different the game was years ago. Every single anecdote the ex-pros told began and ended in the pub. There were tales of drinking at half-time, being so pissed at training that they didn't remember attending at all, and every story inevitably involved a large amount of 'kicking the shit out of' other players, on and off the field. A particularly strange aspect of the evening was the fact that I had to sit on stage with the four former players and have dinner. The 200 fans sat and watched the five of us eat, whilst elevated above them on a stage. In almost complete silence. For an hour. It was like a mental piece of performance art, or a play where all the actors forget their lines but the audience is too polite to say anything. Needless to say, I drank a lot of complimentary Bristolian beer that evening. After the last supper, I did a bit of stand-up for the crowd, who, quite surprisingly, needed some warming up after being sat watching five men eat a three-course meal on a stage for 60 minutes. I was incredibly careful not to ignite any kind of warfare between the Rovers and City supporters, instead choosing to focus on their combined dislike for Gloucester. When it came to the Q&A section, I spent a good hour and a half simply relaying questions from the audience to the pros, who were too far away and way too pissed to hear them. And that was the night.

One of the ex-pros had a couple of seasons with Chelsea in the 70s and as a result had faced a United side that included the legend that is George Best. The very first question from the audience was an enquiry as to what it was like to play against Best. The reply was something along the lines of 'we kicked the shit out of each other on the pitch then got pissed afterwards'. If you wanted to know what it was like to play against Denis Law, coincidentally, they 'kicked the shit out of each other on the pitch then got pissed afterwards'.

Charlie George? Gerry Francis? Trevor Brooking? There was a lot of shit-kicking and pissed-getting.

Imagine if social media had been around in those days? Imagine camera phones capturing and then sharing every pint drunk and punch thrown in pubs up and down the country on Saturday evenings after the games. Social media simply didn't exist as a platform for footballers to get themselves into trouble on. Additionally, social media also didn't exist as a platform for *someone else* to get them into trouble on, because, let's face it, players aren't noshing *themselves* off in hotel rooms on Snapchat. Although I'm sure a fair few have tried.

Unfortunately, footballers on social media aren't all as funny as Crouchy, savvy as Kyle Walker or as hilariously incompetent as Wayne Rooney. As a result, punishments for the mucky or just downright stupid shit that a lot of footballers do can sometimes affect your fantasy team. You can spend hours, *days* even, select yourself a particular in-form midfielder, deciding on him over the dozens of others you had contemplated, only for him to be physically unable to keep his willy off social media. Great. I have to change my team because you can't keep it in your pants, mate. Now, he's looking at being benched this week as punishment, or, even worse, receiving a club-imposed ban, and you're looking at a four-point hit to replace the fool.

In 2016 the internet was awash with footage of Andy Carroll (allegedly) drunk and (allegedly) shouting at (alleged) women while he was (definitely) injured. There have been players – or, we should add the caveat (on our lawyer's strict recommendation) 'people who at least *look like* the players' – filmed doing drugs with ladies of the night, again, in hotel rooms. Out of all these situations that tend to 'leak' on to social media, it's the hotel room that sees the most action. In my next life, I seriously want to come back as a hotel room. Nothing fancy, just three-star or above. Nothing too Travel-Lodgey though, that would be a tough paper round.

Imagine living in a world where people did things privately and *didn't* feel the uncontrollable urge to film the act and share it. I mean, you don't share your toilet breaks with the world, do you? It's an intensely private moment, a time when I truly believe everyone is completely and utterly themselves more than any other occasion in life. I mean, there's probably specialist sites and accounts where you *can* find people sharing their toilet functions, if it's your cup of tea, but the average person would never do that, so why share the other private stuff?

The everyday practices of social media are crazy. It seems to be perfectly acceptable to take a photo of your dinner and post it on Facebook to your 'friends'. But if you were to take the same photo, print it out and actually post it, in the *actual post,* to the same people, some of whom you don't actually know or haven't seen for a decade, then people would think you have problems. Like, serious issues. *I know we only met once, seven years ago at that party of a friend of a friend, but here's a photograph of some spaghetti bolognese I made last Thursday – sorry it's taken so long to get to you, I only had a second-class stamp.*

That is the absurdity of social media, and the sooner footballers – and the rest of us – realise that not everything in this world needs to be recorded, mentioned, noted, commented on and shared through social media, then not only will the world be a happier place, but we won't be having to take points hits to get rid of disgraced players, and we can all go back to kicking the shit out of each other and getting pissed afterwards.

Price changes

Stop me if this sounds at all familiar. *I'm almost certainly going to bring that guy in. I'll just wait until I'm definitely sure about it. Maybe I'll make myself a sandwich while I deliberate. Oh god, decisions decisions. What should I do, what should I do, ham or cheese? No, I'm definitely going to bring him in. Whaaaaaaaat?* While you were eating your ham and cheese sandwich – because you should never need to choose between the two – the player's price rose. It only rose by 0.1 million, but it was enough to ruin things for you. It's the two words that have haunted you since your student days/bus stop cider drinking days: 'Insufficient Funds'. Several thousand other fantasy football managers waited to have their ham and cheese sandwich *after* they transferred that player into their teams. As a result of their punctuality and your tardiness, his price went up and you now can't afford him. The sight of your '-0.1' in the bank, complete with angry red font, as you attempt to perform a transfer is the single worst thing a fantasy football manager can see. The ultimate hellish visual that means there is no hope. No going back. Nothing you can do to right this wrong, this mistake. You can't borrow the money from a relative or a mate at work, you can't explain that you were going to make the transfer 20 minutes ago but didn't because you were busy doing something else. The -0.1 is final. The end of the transaction, the end of all hope.

You now have to compromise. You'll need to bring in a cheaper alternative or sell someone more expensive. God, why had you waited? It was all going to be so perfect. The satisfaction of completing a transfer, or a couple of transfers, and having exactly the right amount of money in the bank really is quite the feeling. Technically, it's better to have a bit of money left in the bank, obviously, but bringing in a couple of players you really want and being able to do so with the *exact* money, like when you pay for a can of Red Bull, some Berocca, packet of Imodium and a bog roll in the corner shop the night after beer and curry night down Wetherspoons and get rid of all your spare change, is incredibly gratifying.

Adversely, there is something to be said for having a few million in the bank whilst at the same time owning a team you are completely happy with. You know it's not real money, but as you glance admiringly at your bank balance, millions and millions of virtual pounds just sat there, unused, un-bloody-wanted if anything, there will be a little smile on your face. That is until, later in the season, when you take too long pulling the trigger on a double transfer and see the dreaded red minus digits in your bank balance. Why hadn't you put a bit aside for a rainy day, damn it?!

Over the course of a season, a player's price will see more peaks and troughs than my recent mountain climbing and pig feeding holiday in Wales, and fantasy football managers will often find themselves trying to anticipate a price rise so they can get in there early. There are so many times I've been sat watching a game, unable to enjoy it because I'm looking at an in-form player, knowing that everyone else is watching him and contemplating getting him in too. *His price is bound to rise isn't it? I should get on board, I won't be able to afford him if it does.* That shouldn't be in the forefront of your mind when watching a player putting on a masterclass, you should be basking in the excellence, appreciating the sweet, sweet art form instead of cursing your own indecisiveness as to whether to bring him in or not. It might be Sunday and the next transfer deadline might be a solid six days away, but everyone else is picking up on how well this kid is playing, you need to bring him in now! Do it! You won't be able to afford him when his price inevitably goes up tonight. Be brave – pull the trigger. He's instantly going to get injured, isn't he?

You will see some managers with astronomical team values after a few months, often several million pounds over the 100 million we all begin with in the fantasy Premier League game. This is because they've started with, or at least *brought in,* players before everyone else, meaning they paid a pittance for them, and they're now worth considerably more. We'd like to state that you don't get anything for having a team that is worth a lot, as we mentioned before, it's not *real* money, you can't pay your water bill with it, or buy a caravan, you can just afford the kind of midfield that we all dream about. We've all seen the guy who wildcards in February and has a middle line consisting of Sterling, Sané, Salah, Mané and Pogba, and we all conclude that he either knows a cheat for the game or he sold his soul to Richard Scudamore in return for an extra five million fantasy football pounds.

Price drops are as impactful on your game as rises, and the two often go hand in hand. You need to ditch an out-of-form or injured player as quickly as you need to jump on an in-form one. Even if he picks up a little knock and is expected to only miss a week, his value will inevitably go down as a few managers get jittery. If the injury is worse than originally thought, more and more will be jumping off that player like rats off a sinking ship, and the next thing you know, you own someone who is now so cheap and useless that it's almost not even worth selling him. You'll have to stick him in that much-maligned last position on your bench and hope that he eventually comes back into his respective team in a month or so. A player's poor form or upcoming fixtures can again be the catalyst for his price fall. He doesn't even need to have been performing badly in footballing terms, someone like N'golo Kanté for instance rarely has a bad spell, but he could be experiencing blanks as far as fantasy football points go. You can hold on to him in the hope he'll turn it around and start bringing in assists and the odd goal, but if he doesn't, then you should have got rid of him sooner, as he's already a lot cheaper than what you bought him for.

A perfect example of price rises and falls is Tottenham's loveable Heung-Min Son. 'Sonny', as he's dubbed by the White Hart faithful, likes to disappear to the Asia Cup every year, missing several weeks of Premier League fixtures. This means, if you don't get rid of him from your squad quickly enough, his price is going to plummet when everyone else realises his considerable price tag could be used to much better effect than having him sat on your bench for weeks on end. However, Son has always proven to be a fantastic fantasy football acquisition, consistently classed and priced as a midfielder, but often played up front by Spurs, and frequently the natural replacement as a centre-forward when Harry Kane gets injured, so as soon as he's back from the Asia Cup, you need to get him in quick! His price will rise again as others begin to cotton on to the fact that he's now a lot cheaper than he was, and bringing him in at his current price is an absolute bargain for the points he returns. If you play it right, you can sell Son at 8.7 million before he goes away and bring him back in at 8.4 when he returns. A fantastic bit of business if you play it right, but, inevitably, we won't, will we? We'll be too busy umming-and-ahhing, second-guessing ourselves, thinking about doing it but not *actually* doing it and eating our ham and cheese fucking sandwiches.

Technology

Human error is a huge part of fantasy football. We, as humans, pick the wrong human goalkeeper and that human goalkeeper lets in five human goals. It happens and there's not much we can do about it. You take it on the chin and in truth you don't mind having a poor week because of errors of judgement like that. Obviously, we blame the humans who are paid tens of thousands of pounds per week rather than us mere mortals who have real-life problems to contend with, but either way it's the kind of problems that feel fair to every person who plays the game. What we can't abide is when uncontrollable third parties stick their nose in and ruin everything. And in fantasy football the part of Yoko Ono is played by technology. It's utterly essential if you want to get into fantasy football but it can stop you in your tracks at any given time. It's merciless, unforgiving and no amount of time on the phone to Virgin Media customer services department will ever get that point across sufficiently.

If *Family Fortunes* were to do a round of 'things people threaten to do but never follow through with' then among the criminal acts and sex stuff you're never brave enough to try would be 'change your internet provider'. Something as trivial as a bad Wi-Fi connection can completely derail your fantasy football week and, while you can't get online to read it, your mates will be crucifying you on the WhatsApp group. Granted, we should be grateful we live in a Wi-Fi age at all and we should also spare a thought for our dial-up forefathers. They not only had to spend an hour trying to get online to change their captain, they also grew up telegraphing when they planned to masturbate to their parents because the house computer sounded like a robot having a stroke when you fired it up. That's no consolation, though, when you leave Glenn Murray in away to Man City because you got sucked in by 'fibre optic', the two most meaningless words in the English dictionary. God forbid you have a job that requires working away and you have to leave your life in the hands of Lenny Henry and his Premier Inn connection. It doesn't seem fair that a game that should be the ultimate leveller is made uneven because some poor sod sees the letters 'GPRS' in the top left corner of his phone.

Technology can also bastardise your team if you happen to be on public transport when you're trying to make changes. We've all been in the scenario where you're sure you hit confirm but apparently Safari disagrees and you don't find out until you log in at home to check your score on a Saturday afternoon. You find yourself making sure you aren't in between two places at 11.30am on a Saturday morning, all because you can't trust the equipment that probably cost you a combined two grand. I've got one friend who even makes sure he doesn't leave to go on holiday on a Saturday. He's convinced his wife he once read that more planes crash on weekends than they do weekdays so it's become second nature for them to fly on a Monday to Friday. That's the kind of messed up genius that is gonna make that lad go far in this game. He is willing to pretend his children's lives might be in danger just so he can shuffle his fictional football team. Credit where it is due, obviously, but it's all irrelevant if we could just put our trust in organisations if they say 'Wi-Fi available' or in our iPhone to have a battery that lasts longer than a Leeds United manager. Throw in forgotten passwords, security questions that mean absolutely nothing to you a decade later and work filters that let you watch Verne Troyer's sex tape but not log into your fantasy football team and all of a sudden you can't think of many reasons to like technology at all. Unless, of course, you really, really like Verne Troyer.

Chris Smalling

Hate is a strong word. I don't hate many things, just the usual stuff – fascism, poverty, Phillip Schofield. I'd like to say at this early juncture that I don't *hate* Chris Smalling, he just did something unforgivable to me, an act so truly horrific that I've never been able to forget. But I won't go as far as to say I feel hatred towards him. However, I would admit that he is certainly up there in the 'have strong feelings of disdain towards' category, alongside people who feel the need to announce when they are 'leaving social media', badly punctuated graffiti and the watery pre-squeeze stuff that comes out of the ketchup bottle and ruins your chips.

What exactly did Christopher Lloyd Smalling do to me that means I burn an effigy of him at midnight under a full moon once a month? He scored an own goal on the very last day of the 2015/16 season, which cost me my work mini-league. Please light a candle for me.

I'd been leading all season. I had done my best to not come across as over confident or cocky, though. No, I was waiting for the final whistle to go first, *then* I was going to unleash furious hell on my colleagues, unbridled mocking and scorn, and I'd choreographed a celebratory dance, composed a small poem and there were going to be many, *many* gifs … But along came Smalling.

Bournemouth are on the attack late in the game, inside the United penalty area, and the ball flies across the face of goal, only for Smalling to stick his stupid foot out and ping it into the back of his own net. He half smiles and raises his eyes as if to say 'what am I like?' I'll tell you what you're like, Chris, you're like a bloody idiot. A bloody idiot who lost me my work mini-league to Ted in accounts. Do you have any idea what it's like to lose to Ted in accounts, Chris? Well, I'll tell you, it's fucking awful. He knows very little about actual football, he just loves a spreadsheet, and he is *the worst* at choreographing and performing celebratory 'I won the work mini-league' dances. Seriously, it was a shambles. Also, to show the full impact of the own goal, it also denied Smalling's team-mate David de Gea the Golden Glove Award for the 2015/16 season, destroying his chances of forever being a small part of history, and some may say that is an even bigger tragedy than me losing my work mini-league.

Chris Smalling is my personal fantasy football nemesis. We all have one. That one player who has hurt you. Maybe his crime against you was five seasons ago, but you've never forgotten. Every time you see his face you will associate it with that disdain. The single time he wronged you will be brought back and the hot bile of loathing will rise up from deep inside you once again. Maybe his indiscretion towards you was relatively minor, maybe it's just been magnified over the years; blown out of proportion and evolved into something so epically atrocious that you will now forever associate him amongst the ranks of Adolf Hitler, your year-seven science teacher Mrs Elliot, and Robbie Savage. Players will score own goals, miss open goals, miss penalties, get sent off and it will have that big, resounding, lasting impact on you. If their one action has made you lose a mini-league, then they would have to do a lot to win you back and return to your good books. Chris Smalling would have to score a goal, regardless of whether it's in the right net this time or not, to directly help me win the entire Fantasy Premier League game for me to forgive him and stop regularly setting fire to the action man I've dressed up in a little Manchester United kit. But, let's be honest, that is as likely to happen as marrying a beautiful glamour model and former page-three girl (insert picture of Chris Smalling standing next to his wife – a beautiful glamour model and former page-three girl).

Whoever your fantasy football arch enemy is, the Moriarty to your Sherlock, the Dr No to your James Bond, the receding hairline to your Steve McClaren, this last entry to the boot room is for you. Stick them in there, banish them from the game of fantasy football for all eternity, for whatever it is that they've done to you. Pull the big lever and get rid of them forever into the abyss as the crowd applauds. It's still absolutely *nothing* like *Room 101*, alright?

*Hands up if you're happy to put your name to a fantasy football board game, but will **definitely** not do any other kind of football related guest appearances in the 90s just to make money.*

TEAM	GW 1	GW2	GW3	GW4	GW5	GW6
Arsenal						
Bournemouth						
Brighton						
Burnley						
Cardiff						
Chelsea						
Crystal Palace	PLEASE					
Everton		HELP				
Fulham			ME			
Huddersfield				I		
Leicester					AM	
Liverpool						LONELY
Man City						
Man Utd						
Newcastle						
Southampton						
Tottenham						
Watford						
West Ham						
Watford						

You'll find this sort of thing on your average fantasy football boffin's hard drive, but we don't recommend looking. Behind every fantasy football expert online is a very, very lonely person crying out for help

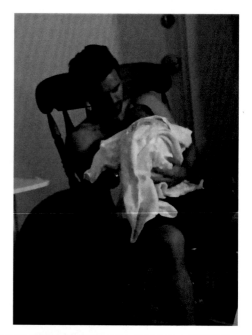

Evan Brady. Evan was willing to miss this moment to choose his back four. What a guy

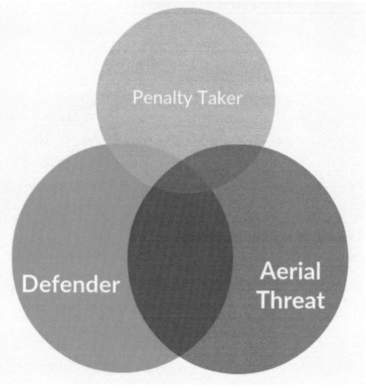

The Unsworth Conundrum. RIP David Unsworth

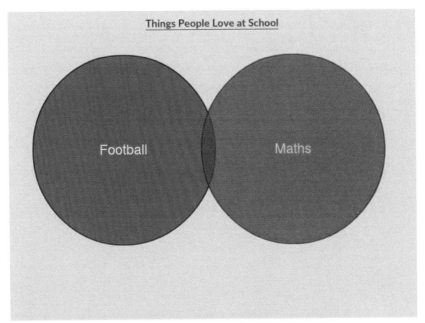

Things People Love at School

Football

Maths

Other things people love at school: Venn diagrams that look like boobs

It's always the way; you run a marathon without doing a single bit of training and your mates jump in right at the end to take some of the glory.

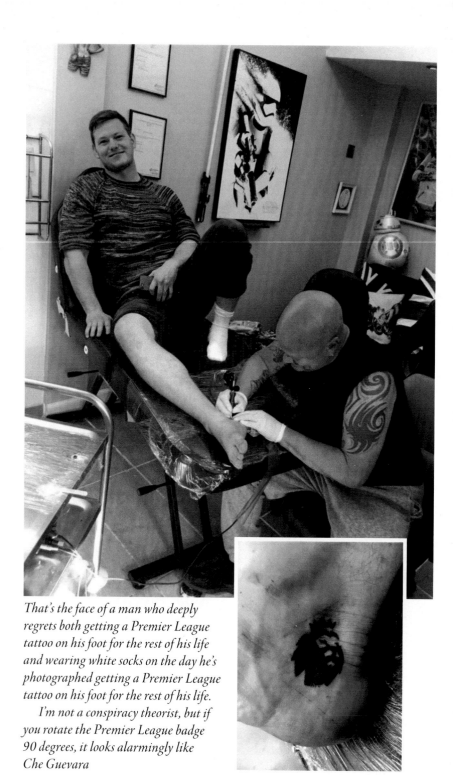

That's the face of a man who deeply regrets both getting a Premier League tattoo on his foot for the rest of his life and wearing white socks on the day he's photographed getting a Premier League tattoo on his foot for the rest of his life.

I'm not a conspiracy theorist, but if you rotate the Premier League badge 90 degrees, it looks alarmingly like Che Guevara

Asmir Begović refuses to pick players he is playing against. Easy at Chelsea. Harder at Stoke

A Creature of Hobbit – Dom Monaghan is a fantasy football regular. Actor Dominic Monaghan looking very serious. We're guessing he just played his Triple Captain.

Having one of our ideas described as 'gash' by Helen Chamberlain is definitely a career highlight.

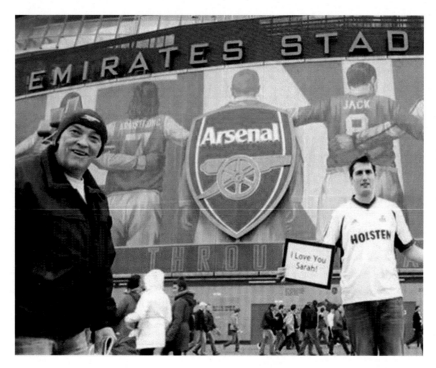

The Luke of Love – Luke McQueen is a fearless comedian, dedicated fantasy football player and hopeless romantic, well, he is an Arsenal fan after all.

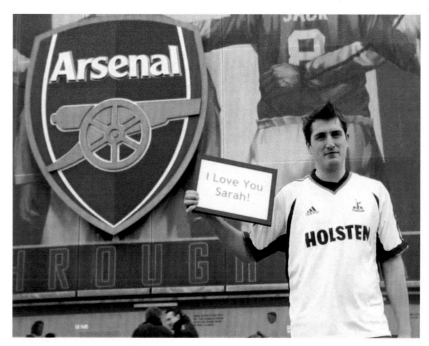

What Are You Playing For?

THE single biggest question you will be asked about your annual insistence on playing fantasy football is 'why?' Why do you bother? Why are you doing this to yourself again? Why was Alfie stood outside the school in the rain until 5pm? In fairness, the *answer* to the last question is 'fantasy football' but it all feeds into that existential crisis you have every July when your partner or less interested friends try to tell you to take a year off. 'Does the general election take a year off?!' was my passionate and irate response to my girlfriend when she tried to coerce me into hanging up my laptop a few years ago. It led to various conversations, not least one in which I realised that I really needed to educate myself on this country's political system if I wanted to continue having a say in how society is governed. I should've used Eurovision as an example, obviously. They're not wrong, though. The question of why we persevere with fantasy football is pretty much embodied by Einstein's famous quote on insanity. Nothing changes and yet year after year we commit to a 38-week course of digital self-harm. It's a whole gestation period, except at the end of it there is no bundle of joy. This need for patience and tolerance of pain over nearly 40 weeks is probably why women are inherently better at playing the game than men. The answer is, I guess, that it isn't fruitless for everyone who plays. Come that glorious day in May, there is one person in every mini-league who has something to show for their hard work. It's not a baby, granted, unless your mini-league has some really fucked up medieval forfeit system. Although read on, you'd be surprised.

Way back when, people used to play fantasy football just for the fun of it, which feels weird because it is essentially just maths and football. And a Venn diagram of people at school who loved both football and maths would show some slim results in the middle. Ideally, we will include yet another Venn diagram below this text, which wasn't something we set out to do, I promise. Before mini-leagues existed you would simply clock up your weekly score and compare with your mates with no competitive element, while trying to be first place in the world. It was a simpler time. It was like winning the 100 metres on school sports day but not getting a medal or any points for Hufflepuff because you weren't as fast as Usain Bolt, even though you were the fastest kid in the school. A title which, looking back, held a weird amount of kudos and power. When would you need it? No one knows, but girls loved it. Weird.

In fact, when I was younger, a jealous mate of mine hit the roof on hearing one of the more popular girls in school fancied me by going bright red and yelling, 'Why? He can't even run!' Safe to say, on hearing this, her affections soon waned. Thankfully, just like horse racing and FIFA before it, fantasy football was corrupted by money, and people soon realised you could run your own league for a fiver each and with it the longest email chain you were ever involved in. As an early example of Machiavellian mind games, my dad used to work for the armed forces and as a result had a pretty hefty email filter. If other members of the league wanted to talk without him knowing they would simply scatter expletives or subject matter of a national concern among the messages and stop him reading them. Turns out, he missed a lot of dinners, a few birthday parties and one major war. Money was, and still is for many, the main incentive when it comes to playing fantasy football. I always think the best amount to play for is to think of an amount that feels slightly uncomfortable. Then double it. Bet you won't miss a deadline now, right? There are variations on just saying the winner gets 20 quid off everyone. One absolutely horrendous-sounding incarnation of financial fantasy stakes is a version that we were made aware of a few years back, which includes pounds per point. When the league ends, you owe anyone who finished above you a pound per point they beat you by. I know! That sounds closer to The Bullingdon Club than it does The Basildon Arms, and definitely not for me. Worse still, the guy who finished top in that league somehow finished top 50 out of five million that year, which earned him thousands. When the other league members arrived home that day, I am sure they were met with a lot of 'why?' Well, that and an application to remortgage.

To agree with Jessie J for a second, though, it really isn't about the money, money, money. And while I have no desire to make the world dance (or do it like the mandem, mandem, although it *does* sound like it could be fun), there is a lot to be said for playing simply for the pride and bragging rights that leave you safe in the knowledge that you are better than your friends. Sure, it is pretty specific in terms of what you are better at. Picking 11 football players who will do well over nine months, like successful sperm. That doesn't stop me for a second, asserting my dominance at any given situation and throwing my previous credits in their face – do you think Kaka would have performed in the Premier League? I'll field this, I am reigning fantasy football champion. Who should play in goal for England? Well, as the current fantasy football champion I think I should answer this one. Anyone know how to fillet a seabass correctly? Fuck off Stuart and put down that lemon, I'm the fantasy football champion, no one touches that fish but me. And that's just with your mates!

You are probably in leagues with your colleagues and bosses. How gratifying will it be when you decimate the woman from the front desk who insists on bringing back traditional hard-boiled sweets when she goes to Menorca and walks her kid round the office and you don't know if you have to take your headphones off and applaud?

Or, even better, your boss! You won't be able to gloat so aggressively or commandeer his seafood, but who needs aggressive when you have passive aggressive? Aggression's much more satisfying, enigmatic, cloaked little brother. You can live off that shit for a full year. After all, you're the current champ until you're not. That's to say, if you are in last place on the eve of game week 38 then who gives a shit? You're still the champ, mate, and you better remind everyone quick sharp. There's also bragging rights to be had closer to home if you want to make day-to-day life awkward. Sure, you can sign up your eight-year-old son or daughter then refuse to help them at any point and deny them internet access whenever you please, but that really is a hollow victory. Why not turn domestic bliss into a unnecessarily stressful existence by taking on your spouse? That's what Isle of Man fantasy football addict Heath Cram did inadvertently during the 2015/16 season. Unbeknown to Heath, his friend and wife conspired and contacted our podcast to say that after ten years of fantasy football dedication, his wife Erin had finally had enough and started playing. Better still, she was beating him. Nothing wrong with losing to your wife, of course, that is unless they hate football and only started playing because they were utterly fed up with the nonsense of it all. 'It was a case of can't beat him, join him. Basically my wife chose fantasy football over divorce' is how Heath describes the origins of the marital rivalry. Not a good start, Heath. As the season progressed, the Crams became more and more competitive, like a really nerdy version of *Mr & Mrs Smith*.

It didn't get any better for Heath, though. 'She soon ended up in the top 50 in the Isle of Man national league,' he told us, half proud, half gutted as Erin took the piss out of both her husband and the subtle patriarchy of her own home country's name. So followed a new family tradition, and Cram-er vs Cram-er became part of the household chores for this once happy couple. In our opinion, they deserve recognition for their dedication to both fantasy football and puns based on 70s movies.

In something that epitomises humankind, however, it soon became clear that there was something more fun than celebrating glory and rewarding excellence. People decided that while they were happy with chucking their 20 quid in the hat for the winner, they wanted something more satisfying, something darker, and, on some occasions, something permanent. Agree with it or not, people wanted to revel in misery and humiliate the weak. And so, forfeits became as much a part of any fantasy football league as prize funds or winner's dinners. In fairness, there is method to the masochism. The problem with any competition that lasts as long as a football season is that there comes a point when those suffering at the bottom realise they aren't going to win and soon lose interest. Think Derby County in the 2007/08 season or those types who pretend not to care once they start losing and suddenly decide 'it's for squares anyway' even though you know they record *Tipping Point* daily and still check every post box they walk past to see if it's ER, GR or VR. These people need consequences for their ineptitude and apathy. Just how severe these consequences become really depends on the mindset of those involved and the strength of their friendship.

Over the years, we've heard some frankly outrageous mini-league forfeits, and it only seems fitting to share some with you, in case any of you needed inspiration for how to damage lifelong relationships with people you've loved for many years. For most of us, last place could mean buying dinner for those above them or treating everyone to a night out. I've always liked it in pub quizzes when second-to-last place gets a bottle of wine, just to incentivise people who might want to give up. That way no one gets their feelings hurt, right? However, it seems the go-to emotion for most fantasy players is humiliation, and while a slap-up curry on the house is all well and good, what's the point if I don't see one of my oldest friends have an anxiety attack? Football fans are weird. Many fans see their mini-league as an opportunity to pretend they're on *Impractical Jokers*, with one of last season's most common league forfeits being performance based. Astonishingly, there were several examples of leagues that signed the loser up to an open mic comedy night and went to watch them perform. While some allowed them to deliver their own 'material', the real genius came in the scenarios where the league winners provided the jokes on the night of the gig. Better still, one instance laid claim to sending the loser up there with a blank bit of paper where a fully written set was meant to be. As two people who are pretty clued up within the comedy circuit, the truth is that they won't have been worse than many a 'comedian' we have gigged with in the past, but it's enough to give you heart palpitations for the best part of the year. Obviously, there's the less traumatic options of just making them do a photo shoot in their rival's team shirt, something I made my co-author Tom do a few years back. Or you can find an innovative, hipster, *woke* way to punish the league loser, which describes one of my favourites from last year, where a group of workmates insisted last place had to ask on social media for his friends and colleagues to sign his petition that the world was flat. That's some serious high-brow shit and one for the pseudo-intellectuals among us. It's a great avenue of uncharted humiliation, though. Imagine having to declare your love for *Mrs Browns Boys* on a weekly basis or apply to be on *The Apprentice* until you got on. It's a genius all of its own. However, sometimes it's the outright weird that wins out, and if you look hard enough online you'll unearth examples that include an overweight man recreating the entirety of a Selena Gomez music video. It's a very niche category on pornhub, but you'll find it eventually. And it is definitely in this 'weird' category where our next example of fantasy football failure falls.

Manchester United fan David Rawlinson made the mistake of being rubbish at fantasy football in 2016 and was immortalised by his 'friends' as he went viral in the most peculiar of situations. A league that started with the loser buying dinner evolved into making poor David, a financial analyst and grown adult, busk in the city centre, dressed as a nun, on the clarinet. It's hard as you read that sentence to work out where the punishment peaks, isn't it?

My original suspicion was that Dave must've lost a fantasy football league when he was seven or eight years old that meant he had to learn the clarinet, but it would appear that he did that voluntarily, which will have at least prepared him for fantasy football making him unattractive to the opposite sex. Armed with boards saying 'THIS IS MY PUNISHMENT FOR LOSING LAST YEAR'S FANTASY FOOTBALL LEAGUE' and 'DO NOT GIVE ME MONEY, I AM A DISGRACE', David took to the busy streets of Manchester and went at it dressed as a nun to give the people woodwind. Who knows? Maybe the second board came in handy throughout the year. The video of David soon went viral and he told the *Manchester Evening News,* 'I didn't touch my team for about two months so I was always struggling'. Now, I don't know about you but I'm starting to have my suspicions about Dave. Let's look at the evidence so far. He's a bloke who owns both a clarinet and a nun's outfit and decided to take two months off the game. Unless those months were June and July, mate, then I think you just fancied a stint as Sister Mary Clarinet. Either way, it's an excellent example of just how bizarre a league forfeit can get when it's your closest friends.

If you're looking for something less bizarre and more potentially life threatening then look no further than Ian McNamara from across the pond in Cincinnati. Not only did Americans invent fantasy football, but there's a very good chance they invented league forfeits if Ian's group of friends is anything to go by. In their infinite wisdom, Ian and his comrades decided that the loser of their league would run a marathon. Now, some people love marathons. Every year you see Gordon Ramsay on the BBC doing the London marathon, stopping for interviews presumably in an attempt to get four hours away from his 74 children. Then there's the idiots dressed as pantomime horses or kitchen appliances to raise money for charity, although you get the feeling they'd do it just to tell everyone they've ever met. For them it wouldn't be a punishment, but what about if they didn't do any training? That's right, Ian McNamara holds the dubious honour of running 26 miles with absolutely no training. On hearing that level of dedication to age-old fantasy football traditions, we knew we had to catch up with the world's least likely Mo Farah and had a chat with Ian.

First up, we wanted to know how it got to this. If a man is running a marathon for losing a mini-league, there must have been some bad shit in his past. Any therapist would know that. 'The first year, someone had to poop their pants in front of the group.' Well that answers that. It's as simple as it is beautiful, and I don't think any one act has ever summed up the stupidity and prehistoric simplicity of men as a gender. A group of guys sat round watching their friend literally shit their pants just because it's funny. I won't lie. I love fantasy football as much as the next nerd, but if I had to run a marathon without training then I'd probably fancy a year off for both my sanity and my legs. Ian is a sucker for punishment though, and when we asked him if he considered a fantasy sabbatical, he was pretty forthright with his answer – 'Absolutely not. This is one of the highlights, if not *the* highlight of our entire year. And because everyone in the league is a close childhood friend, despite the punishment being absolutely unbearable, this league provides an excellent outlet to stay connected with friends despite living in different cities all across the globe. The league is a blessing and a curse.' Annoyingly, he's right. Only a group of really close friends could turn this level of chaos and absurdity into a heart-warming way to grow closer. I'm picturing the movie already: *Fantasy Foes*, starring Vince Vaughn, Will Ferrell, the Wilson brother who doesn't have a nose that looks like a foot and Jonah Hill. Before you start to think it's cute though, remember the bit where you found out they watched their mate defecate fully clothed. You'd forgotten, hadn't you? (That's definitely going to be the Jonah Hill character.) Also, spare a thought for Ian's family! Busking and stand-up comedy is embarrassing for sure, but they won't kill you! Every year you hear tragic stories about people quite literally dying whilst attempting to run a marathon, and these people at least went for a jog beforehand! What do Ian's nearest and dearest think of this insanity? 'My family hates it. When they found out I lost and would be running the marathon, they were sincerely concerned for my safety. They also don't like the attention we get for it.' Oops. Sorry about that Mr and Mrs McNamara. Don't feel too sorry for Ian, though, he brought a lot of it on himself. With the punishments decided by the boys before the season starts, he could have prepared for the worst. However, Ian decided pride was more important than losing one or both of his legs and/or lungs. 'Once I found out I'd be the one running, it became an issue of pride. I came to the conclusion I was absolutely not going to finish, so I would at least not embarrass myself by training and failing. If I was going to fail, I was going to fail with pride, the pride of a stubborn and obstinate aging man, past his prime, clinging to youth. In fact, I became honour bound not to train, often bragging that I didn't need to train at all.' If that doesn't sum up a fantasy football league then I don't know what does (Ian is definitely being played by Ferrell). It shows the lengths friends will go to to ensure people don't lose interest and just how much we love to put each other through hell. Astonishingly, Ian surprised himself and left his friends dumbfounded by somehow completing the gruelling run in a time of five hours 58 minutes, just two minutes before the organisers were going to end the race. This guy must absolutely love football to put himself through this just for the love of the game, right? Well, actually, no not really. 'I personally do not enjoy one second of watching football.' Come to think of it, that makes sense Ian, you incredible lunatic.

It might not have felt like it for Ian at the time, but at least a marathon has an end date when the only thing that remains is the memory and the scars from the blisters. The same cannot be said for West Ham fan Shaun Coveley's frankly terrifying mini-league. Shaun and his mates got fed up with people quitting mid-season and decided to make the repercussions slightly more permanent. When we asked him to tell us a bit about his league, it was a tale as old as time. That is, until the bit where he mentions permanently scarring your body. 'The league started as most others do, just for fun and bragging rights, but after many years of that it became a bit tedious. Someone suggested a forfeit and a few ideas were bandied around. I'd like to say that we started with something more gentle than a tattoo and it was built up to, but once a tattoo was mentioned everything else seemed tame in comparison.' That's right. Shaun's mates decided that the loser of each year's league deserved to have their shame inked on them for all eternity. What tattoo are they forced to get? The Premier League logo, of course. 'Currently there's 18 teams in the league, which is up on the previous two years. Obviously people are keen to get the Premier League logo tattooed on them,' Shaun told us, which really does make you wonder about the mindset of all of us who love to hate this game so much. Our first thought was that surely someone has backed out. I don't know about you, but I think my integrity would be tested if I was putting my skin in Phil Jones's hands. These guys don't have that luxury. 'Backing out isn't an option.' Shaun explained. 'On the last game week, we all meet in the pub and watch the scores come in. The tattoo is booked about an hour after the games finish, so we drag the loser straight there and there's no time to reconsider.' By 'no time to reconsider' Shaun means, 'no fucking way we'd let him reconsider'. There's always *time* to reconsider! That time, we presume, is spent with four of your closest friends taking an arm or a leg each and strapping you to a bed, like prison officers do when they carry out the death penalty. Shaun himself has managed to avoid the tattoo, which is the non-physical badge of honour you want from that league. He did tell us about when he and his mates came up with the idea though, and it takes the honour right out of love, honour and obey. 'The tattoo was agreed a few hours into a friend's wedding, so I don't think we would have all been thinking particularly clearly. There were a few options but it needed to be extreme enough to keep everyone's interest for the season, so we all decided on that, including Chris the groom. Chris ended up losing that year, so he'd agreed to a Premier League tattoo on his wedding day, for better or for worse.' That's where the added layer of this punishment hits you. The partners! Will somebody please think of the partners? Don't feel sorry for these idiots. They chose to potentially have a corporate logo etched on them permanently. Their other halves and families didn't sign up for this! There is a slight upside though, as Shaun explains. It does get your football-hating spouse suddenly interested. 'It's hard not to get invested in it when your partner's permanently scarring themselves with a fantasy football tattoo. So it was nice to hear one player's wife, when we went out for dinner, stating, "He just keeps moaning about Aaron Wan-Bissaka's bonus points."' It's these kinds of stakes that suddenly turn a pastime into an obsession, and I think we can all relate, to an extent. We've all been in a meeting when you stare at your boss so long that his head turns into that of Gabriel Jesus and you have to stop yourself asking him if he is likely to start on Wednesday. It's all consuming at the best of times, which begs the question, for Shaun and his friends, is it even still fun? 'It's definitely fun when you're safe from the forfeit,' he says, in a way only a guy with a blank canvas for skin can, 'but when you're down there you can't think of much else. Someone in our league is a professional lower league football scout, but that doesn't seem to translate to fantasy football. He describes it as "ruining 38 weeks of the year". You find yourself watching Huddersfield vs Fulham hoping for a 0-0. One mate, Harris, ran the London marathon this year. He stopped a few hours in to ask if Vardy had scored. Safe to say it's taken over his life.' We should add that Harris ran the marathon voluntarily and with, we assume, at least having a regular brisk walk a week or two before. Once Shaun has read Ian's story, though, who knows what next year will bring. One thing is for sure, however, these boys take this shit seriously. 'People are always trying to psych each other out and get them to take an unnecessary hit, whether it's making up rumours of a long-term injury or telling them that their premium striker has just put in a transfer request.' It's hard not to admire that level of dedication to shithousery and winning. If you're willing to get a tattoo then you're definitely willing to stoop to all manner of levels of deceit in order to win. Well, that and to make sure you just include someone in the league who isn't as good as you. Shaun is lucky enough to have one of those people in his life. 'One of our mates, Phil, has a wobble every year. The pressure gets to him and he makes outrageous picks in the hope that Jason Puncheon scores from 35 yards. It never works and he ends up taking eight-point hits at the start of a game week, before inevitably finishing low down. He's managed to avoid the tattoo so far, but after a -12 in order to get in Calum Paterson this week, it's looking more and more likely.' Once you speak to Shaun you realise they're just a bunch of guys who really bloody love fantasy football and they seem to have a hell of a lot of fun playing it, even more than those who don't have such a huge axe swinging over their head. Plus, it's only a tattoo. What's the real harm in that? Well, Shaun can tell you that. 'About an hour after the first tattoo was done, someone mentioned that it looked like the UKIP logo, which isn't something they'd want to be associated with. So they're always quite eager to clear that one up sharpish.' OK, but other than people thinking you're a bigot just because you're awful at fantasy football, what's the harm in that?

At the pinnacle of all these punishments, above the marathons, catholic woodwind fetishes and tattoos, is a terrifying Irish-based organisation (don't panic, not that one) called the Forfeit League. They've become somewhat part of fantasy folklore (probably the name of another podcast) and joining their league should come with a medical. These ten brave souls live by the mantra 'if you're not last, you're first', and nothing could better sum up the despair of losing any mini-league, let alone theirs. The Forfeit League really couldn't care less who ends up on top, or if you extended your lead by ten points last week. Like when someone shouted 'bundle' at school, as long as you're not bottom then you've got every reason to be happy. On their website, they profess to be 'average at fantasy football' but that they take it 'very, very seriously'. You'll see why. They also explain that the strategy behind not losing is very different to that of attempting to be victorious because they're all 'terrified of the risks associated with trying to win'. It's one hell of a point. If you're in a league where the consequences of losing outweigh the rewards of winning, then who cares if you don't make an early transfer or avoid the punt on the new Ecuadorian up front for Leicester? It's also this kind of self-credited understanding of economics and risk/reward that makes us all believe we are essentially qualified to be hedge fund managers. Only this isn't other people's money so it's *way* more important. The Forfeit League (which we'd normally abbreviate to TFL but don't want to mislead people that London's tube drivers only strike in order to play fantasy football) operate a monthly forfeit for the player in last place at the end of every month, and to be honest some of them are worse than most people put in place for their overall punishment. Being last at these calendar checkpoints can lead to you having your legs waxed, singing Christmas carols on your own in a city centre or forced to endure fancy dress chosen by league rivals. It's basically every nightmare stag do you've ever tried to avoid or attend, depending on your penchant for horrendous forced fun. The stress of direct debits can be enough to make the end of the month unenjoyable, let alone having to contend with the possibility of explaining to your colleagues why you've got no eyebrows while dressed as an inflatable penis. Your legs would look great, at least. And that's just the *monthly* forfeits. At the end of the season, these punishment pioneers head to the pub and send the league's bottom three to separate European destinations. You weren't expecting that were you? All of a sudden it makes you yearn for a leg wax and *Away in a Manger*. The bottom three are given a list of ten tasks to complete and a boarding pass, and on arriving at their mystery cities they must turn back around and race home to the pub, while the winners, or *non-losers*, enjoy their day. Now, we've all landed at a European hotspot and wanted to come straight back home. It's every Club 18–30 holiday anyone has ever been on, but for losing a fantasy football league it's a bit fucking much, isn't it? Well, being the bloody good guys that they are, the Forfeit League tend to tie in this epic finale with some fundraising for local charities, although I'm almost certain that's partly to ease your own conscience for sending your mate to Bratislava dressed a schoolgirl. After an elaborate point-scoring system and everyone's safe return to the pub, the overall loser is then subjected to a shoe-based drinking forfeit which, in truth, feels slightly underwhelming when you've been through customs twice that same day. Their dedication, however, to keeping their fantasy football league interesting for a full term is pretty admirable, even if a little sadistic. Now, go and hug your best friend and tell them you love them. They're not that bad after all.

Inside the Dressing Room

IN a game that is played by so many millions of people across the globe, it is inevitable that some of those players will be famous. Fame is a subjective concept nowadays; you can become famous for eating a pie during a televised FA Cup game or putting salt on someone's food in an extravagant manner. But there are a handful of people who play fantasy football who are genuinely and – slightly more justifiably – well known.

The name Nikolaj Coster-Waldau may not ring any instant bells, and maybe you're trawling through your mind for which Premier League team he had a term with. Was it Middlesbrough back in the days of Fabrizio Ravanelli? However, Nikolaj Coster-Waldau is, in fact, better known as keen incest practitioner Jaime Lannister from some little television show called *Game of Thrones*. Nikolaj is a keen fantasy Premier League player, even going as far as to tweet

Harry Kane in the penultimate game week of the 2017/18 season, wishing him luck, as he'd used his triple captain chip on the Spurs striker, at home to Newcastle.

'*@nikolajcw: @HKane just sending you lots of positive goalscoring karma. My fantasy football season depends on some kane magic. Saved my triplecapt for this week. Come on HARRYYY*'

Kane scored the only goal of the game, which isn't a brilliant haul when using one's triple captain chip, but it's better than a blank, so perhaps Nikolaj owes Kane; let's just hope he *does* always pay his debts. Maybe if the actor had made better use of the 280 characters which had been available to him on Twitter since the previous November, then he might have been able to come up with something a bit more inspiring for Mr Kane. Although, to be fair, one of his hands is made of actual gold, so we'll cut him some slack on his unnecessarily brief tweet.

Another well-known figure who, funnily enough, rose to prominence amongst the fantasy footballing community in the exact same game week as 'The Song of Kane and Jaime', was England cricketer Stuart Broad. As well as previously going out with Neil's sister from *The Inbetweeners* in real life (if you know, you know, if you don't, Google), Broady can also boast a decent fantasy Premier League resume, being the highest scorer in 2017/18's game week 37 with a whopping 169 points! Howzat? Pretty bloody good.

Other celebrities who play fantasy football include large *Pointless* host and king of the stats Richard Osmond, enthusiastic Scottish tennis 'personality' Andy Murray and actor Dominic Monaghan from *Lord of the Rings, Lost,* that Eminem music video where he gets off with Megan Fox, and an absolutely barnstorming fantasy football podcast called *The Gaffer Tapes.* Those who play fantasy football come from all walks of life, but there's something almost validating when you hear that an accomplished actor, sportsman or entertainer sits there and wastes a shitload of time picking their team and organising their bench just like we do. And if there's one thing that we as grownups desperately need when we're inputting the attacking returns of Leicester defenders into a data spreadsheet, it's validation that we're not losers and/or just a little bit weird. Just keep telling yourself that Monaghan got off with Megan Fox, mate.

Of course, the majority of famous fantasy football managers are made up of footballers themselves. Whether they are still playing or retired pros, nothing fascinates and excites us mere fantasy footballing mortals more than hearing a real-life footballer plays the game, just like us. As soon as a footballer, especially one featured in the actual game itself, is mentioned, several very important and interesting questions arise: Do they pick themselves? Do they pick their team-mates? Do they pick their rivals? Do they pick this week's opponents? It's a minefield of intriguing questions that we endeavour to answer.

In 2017 we were asked to be guests on Bournemouth goalkeeper Asmir Begovic's 'Season of Sport' podcast to talk fantasy football. It was very interesting to hear the former Chelsea shot-stopper talk about being a keen player of the game. There was, of course, no way we could appear on Asmir's show and not mention the fact that the keeper scored for Stoke against Southampton in 2013, which would have had huge ramifications for anyone who had him in their fantasy football team that week. A goalkeeper who scores a goal must be the ultimate haul of fantasy football points, we thought, only to find out from the man himself that he received a measly six points for his efforts. Six points?! The same as a defender would receive if he'd scored! Far be it for us to criticise the absolute institution that is the fantasy Premier League game, but an utter minimum of a dozen points should be awarded for a goalkeeper who manages to score a goal, surely. Keepers are a lot less than twice as unlikely to score as a defender, so a *bare minimum* of twice the points should be allocated if they did manage to pull off the highly improbable and score a goal.

We sat down with Asmir again to talk about his relationship with fantasy football in a little more depth, and it was pretty evident straight away that even the pros have the same headaches as us. The first thing we wanted to know from Asmir – apart from how we could become as tall and attractive as he is – is how many professional footballers he believes play fantasy football. It had always intrigued us as to how many pros have one eye on how the players around them are scoring. 'I would say that around 50 per cent of professionals play the game,' the beautiful Bosnian told us, 'could be more, but from my experience I would say that is a safe bet.'

With Asmir's estimated half of pros playing fantasy football, it throws up some compelling questions, and the very first we wanted to know was whether these players pick themselves. Surely it's the ultimate in ego to select yourself in your own fantasy football team, but Mr Begovic maintains he doesn't partake in the act of self-love, or at least doesn't admit to it. On the subject of whether he has ever picked himself over the years, Asmir laughs, 'Normally I don't. I have only selected myself once in my draft league.' Modest *and* handsome.

So his own name won't be on his team sheet, unlike many pros we've heard of, but who else can't the big man bring himself to pick? 'I always take out the players I am playing against. I never want those guys to do well when we play them, of course.' *Loyal*, modest and handsome, we bloody hate him. It is admirable, as well as interesting, that Asmir is clearly worried about a potential for his allegiances to be tested, as the likes of Sergio Agüero steamrollers towards him one-on-one. He doesn't want any kind of doubt in his mind – there's no '*Oh well, if he does score at least I'm getting four fantasy points*'. That kind of talk won't console your team-mates in the dressing room afterwards: '*Yes, I understand we lost, boys, but it's not all bad news*'.

It is a wonder whether other pros pick their opposition. Perhaps some of them select that week's foes for the same reason as the guy who bets against his own team: so that if they lose it softens the blow a little bit. Asmir is the consummate professional, however, and his reply to our question of if he ever checks his fantasy football score at half-time was rightfully a resounding no. Granted, we wanted him to say that he's straight down the tunnel and instantly logging into his team to see how they're faring after 45 minutes, or maybe to see where he himself is at in the bonus-point system. But alas, 'My focus is always on the game and my fantasy team gets checked after the game, always.' Surely, if you're playing a really shit team, you'd be tempted to keep your phone next to the goalpost, wouldn't you? So that when the ball inevitably ends up down the other end of the field for the majority of the game, you can have a few quick refreshes of your score, maybe a swift tinker, have a look at who you should bring in next week, or perhaps even a cheeky little hypothetical wildcard, you know? I mean, that's if the opposition are *really* shit. I know I would. I'm *always* playing fantasy football at work.

It's a valid point, though. For tens of thousands of us, we need that day job and those hours sat in front of a computer just to get our fantasy football admin done. Because if I'm forced by my other half to go on bloody holiday, then I just know I'm not going to get the right amount of fantasy footballing hours in, and as a result it's going to be evident in my score for the duration of the 'holiday'. Asmir, like all professionals, always gets to go on holiday when there's no football on. What are the chances?! Lucky buggers. We asked Asmir how much time he was able to give to fantasy football, what with being an actual footballer with a job that is monitored a lot closer and by a few more people than the rest of us. I mean, it's not like he can walk around holding a piece of paper, pretending to be busy, then disappear for a sit-down wee for half an hour – I think one or two people in the crowd might notice. 'I try and make sure I am following things regularly and keep my team updated, but sometimes everyday life gets in the way of that, of course.' The way Asmir finishes the sentence with 'of course' alludes to the fact he assumes we too find that everyday life gets in the way of fantasy football. Obviously, we nodded knowingly as if in agreement, as if we had actual lives like he does, that could 'get in the way' of fantasy football, but in all honesty, other than being in some kind of coma, nothing gets in the way of fantasy football. I mean, other than all the training, press conferences, meetings with sponsors, autograph signings, TV interviews, friends, families and celebrity parties, but we're all doing that shit, right?

On the subject of celebrity, we asked Asmir who the most famous person in his mini-league was. 'Good question!' he begins, 'I always think that you guys from The Gaffer Tapes are quite famous people to play against. It's always nice to test yourself against the best.' Loyal, modest, handsome *and* a bloody good judge of character. Cheers Asmir, your cheque is in the post, mate.

We wanted to know who Asmir plays his fantasy football against. As well as being part of our own (not so) mini-league, we asked whether he is part of a mini-league with any players from his current Bournemouth side: 'We generally have a league every year between all members from the club.' But you won't find any crazy, irresponsible or testicle-retractingly embarrassing forfeits at Dean Court: 'It's usually about pride, and the banter that flies around makes it always worthwhile.' We've read between the lines there and can only assume that 'banter' is clearly code for a brand-new Aston Martin, a fortnight's use of the third home in the South of France and a backrub in the showers. God, I bet he's got a lovely back.

However, fantasy football is the great leveller – all animals are equal when it comes to the game. You can be as loyal, handsome, modest, good a judge of character and as able to score from your own penalty area as you like, but there's no special treatment, no favourites amongst the fantasy football gods. We asked Asmir for his phone number. He said no. So we asked him instead what his worst fantasy football decision was, just to make ourselves feel better about ourselves. 'It's never good when you pick the wrong person as captain. I have triple captained a player once, who came on for 10 minutes and gave me three overall points, so moves like that I am not very proud of!' Well, you should be proud Asmir. Be proud that you've won the Premier League with Chelsea, be proud that you've represented your country over 60 times, be proud you scored from 97.5 yards, but, most of all, be proud, be really, *really* proud, that you know us because we're celebrities and 'the best', as you said, and once you've said it you can't go back, so there.

Other footballers who have been known to dip their highly skilled toes into the green-and-red-arrowed waters of fantasy football include Crystal Palace's Patrick van Aanholt, who not only plays the game, but hosted one of the biggest mini-leagues in the world in the 2018/19 season. 'The League of Doing Bits' was the most popular mini-league when the season began; an absolute must-join for tens of thousands of managers. Van Aanholt's own campaign started on an incredibly positive note, too, getting an assist, a clean sheet and a couple of bonus points on the first weekend.

The fantasy football team of Cardiff keeper Neil Etheridge appeared online in the second game week of the 2018/19 season, and it was revealed that he had indeed picked himself but decided that he only deserved a spot on his own bench. In a huge act of modesty Etheridge instead gave United's David de Gea the nod, a move that backfired drastically as de Gea pulled in a meagre two points, whereas Etheridge not only got a clean sheet, but saved a penalty, pulled out half a dozen saves and was awarded all three bonus points, amassing a whopping 16 in total! The pros tend to be in mini-leagues with other pros – it's elitist like that – and Etheridge is in a league with his former Fulham team-mate Chris Smalling, who is also in a mini-league with his current Manchester United colleagues. The United boys had their teams 'leaked' online, although I don't know how much actual leakage occurred. It's not like when naked photos of celebrities appear on the internet as a result of highly illegal and immoral invasions of privacy, which, incidentally, can be completely avoided by simply not being so fucking narcissistic as to simply *have* to take photographs of yourself naked all the time, you big-headed cretins. No, I can only assume someone knew someone who knew someone who knew one of the United lads were in a league with a mate of a mate and could look at their team and subsequently the mini-leagues they are in, that way. It's hardly hacking Jennifer Lawrence's iCloud, which, as I said, is completely immoral, corrupt and wrong, and, as a result, none of us have ever laid eyes on those pictures as a matter of principle.

Luke Shaw had the maximum of three Manchester United players in the draft of his team that turned up online, although not picking himself; instead he plumped for David de Gea, Paul Pogba and Andreas Pereira, whereas Chris Smalling only had de Gea, while Phil 'Judas' Jones didn't have a single United team-mate at all! Interestingly, and diehard Man United fans will have to cover their ears for this bit, all three of the players decided to go heavy on Liverpool and – gasp – Manchester City players.

Ex-pros are getting in on the game as well. The fact that they are more used to the swively leather pundit's chair than the football pitch nowadays doesn't matter, they're still keeping involved as far as fantasy is concerned. In fact, the majority of the footballers of yesteryear can be found in one place – no, not the bar at the golf club in ill-fitting polo shirts, but the *PL Pundits v Presenters* mini-league. You'll find the likes of Alan Shearer, Phil Neville and Ian Wright taking on James Richardson and Jules Breach. A special shout-out must be conducted for former Manchester United and Denmark goalkeeping legend Peter Schmeichel, not only for picking his son Kasper, but for the outrageously good team name: 'Zenit St-Peters Heard'. He should win the mini-league on that alone.

There's also those recognisable names that juxtapose as you trawl through the league names. Recognisable but out of place are those celebrity fans who might live a lavish lifestyle that we can't relate to, while we fish a child's shit out of the bath or mutter that the neighbours leave their bins out for days at a time, but they love fantasy football in the same way we do. It's the ultimate leveller. Their millions of Instagram followers and soy diet won't help them have a better Saturday afternoon than you. To clarify, they will almost certainly have a better Saturday afternoon than you, but for that brief moment when the bonus points drop, you can be better than that guy you saw on telly. Celebrity football fans are nothing new. Cameras at live games can't wait to cut to Russell Brand pretending to be normal, sat in with the West Ham fans, or Rod Stewart up at Celtic draped in something utterly age inappropriate. Penny Lancaster I think her name is. Celebrity fantasy football fans are a bit of a rarer breed and we suspect that's because, and we hate to break it to you, it's just not very cool. I'm not sure how we got to a place in society where teeth whitening sponsorship deals and having avocado on absolutely fucking everything is cool and fantasy football isn't, but here we are. So, celebrities aren't always vocal about their love of the game in the same way we are. That's why it's so great when one raises their head above the parapet and says 'yes, I got off with Megan Fox in an Eminem music video but leave me alone, I've got to check if Deulofeu got the assist'. Step forward actor and fantasy football superfan Dominic Monaghan. In a bizarre turn of events, we ended up on a night out with Dom in a London-based martial-arts themed video game bar, which seemed the perfect setting to find out more about his football habits. It might seem an unfair advantage for Dom. After all, a guy who has been in all three *Lord of The Rings* films knows a thing or two about fantasy, but he does have to contend with being a 'soccer' fan in America. It's hard enough hearing them pronounce 'aluminium' but he also has to contend with time difference and deadlines. 'If I want to check team sheets, I will usually have to wake up at 4.30am,' Dom tells us. 'But I'm often up at 5am anyway for the first game of the weekend.' That's some serious dedication to your line-up. Although, we also suspect he is up at that time hitting the gym and shotting wheatgrass. You need to be pretty trim if you're going to be getting off with Megan Fox in music videos. Dom can often be found in an undisclosed pub in Los Angeles, in his Man United shirt watching the goals, and hopefully points, roll in. Don't be fooled by the showbiz location, though, he takes this shit seriously. 'I'll always crunch the stats on the app for player comparisons. Essentially, I look at how many transfers I have, and how much money that will give me. From there I pick the position I think warrants the most money, then I check form and fixtures for at least three to four weeks ahead.' Sounds a bit less showbiz now, doesn't he? Like most of us, Dom wants to win and you've got to be meticulous if you want to take home your mini-league. Plus, he is a creature of hobbit after all. Whenever I read about a Hollywood actor or millionaire pop star playing fantasy football, I tend to console myself with the fact that they must get so busy that they simply don't have time to give their team the attention it deserves. As soon as a big job comes along, their team goes to shit, surely. Dom annoyingly debunks that myth pretty quickly. 'Being on film sets you tend to have enough free time to check your team. It's harder for me when I'm working with wild animals.' It's important to clarify here that a) this isn't a *Star Wars* spoiler and b) he isn't referring to that time he got off with Megan Fox in that Eminem video. Dom has his own wildlife series called *Wild Things with Dominic Monaghan*. 'Quite often I am camping in an isolated area with no service for three or four weeks. For this I pick a "set and forget captain" and make sure I have a strong bench. It's not ideal but it's always fun to check once I leave the jungle.' Maybe we can't all relate to the leaving the jungle part, but the 'set and forget captain' is a phrase-coining that we are on board with. The fantasy football equivalent of putting your out of office on. When you speak to a celebrity, though, you mainly just want to know what famous people they're in a league with, right? Luckily, Dom knew exactly what we were getting at and got straight to it. 'Yes, I'm in a *Star Wars* mini-league. Currently 11th out of 250.' That's all we wanted to hear, mate. Unprompted and likely unwanted, we then proceeded to suggest the following team names: 'The Empire Strikes Back Four', 'Return of the Jedinak', 'A New (Nick) Pope', 'Luke KyleWalker', 'The Phantom Denis (Irwin)'. If any of you happen to get a job on the next *Star Wars* film, we strongly advise you to use any of these names or contact us for more – available for 20 galactic credits each. After making it abundantly clear that he would never hold up filming to activate his wildcard and that he loved his job, Dom did tell us that he has now and then spoken to the players at United about fantasy football and done that thing we've all fantasised about doing. 'I've told Rashford and Pogba to get a hat-trick when I've captained them before! They look at me like I'm deranged.' I can't tell you the amount of times I've imagined myself giving my boys a pep talk before a game, but it's good to know that it has zero effect in person too. And, for the record, Dom, that look isn't a deranged look. It's a look that says 'can't believe that guy got off with Megan Fox in that Eminem video'. We've all been there.

We wanted the hot take on fantasy from a football broadcasting legend, someone we have looked up to both metaphorically from a career perspective and physically from our living room floor on a hungover Saturday morning. Someone who hosted the weekend staple, the cult footballing institution that is *Soccer AM,* for an astonishing 22 years: Helen Chamberlain. We asked Hells Bells, first and foremost, if she had ever been a fantasy player, knowing full well that if she wasn't, it would be the quickest interview since Sky's Rob Palmer called Harry Redknapp a wheeler-dealer.

'Yes, I have been a fantasy player!' – phew – 'In fact I was borderline obsessed with it years ago.' We wondered just how long ago, and luckily we weren't disappointed. 'I am old enough to remember when it was a new thing. I think it started in *The Telegraph*, that's the one I first heard of. Everyone did it from a big list in the paper; there were lots of crossings out and pencil marks everywhere. I took it so seriously I'd not get my entry in until the deadline as I'd still be fiddling about with it.' Ah, showing the traits of a good fantasy football manager there, tinkering right up until the deadline. Although I assume it was slightly different, as nowadays you can tamper and fiddle on your phone or laptop until 11.29 am on a Saturday, one minute before the deadline, but surely in the good old days you had to worry about slow posties and second-class stamps.

So, we're back in the retro days of fantasy football with Hells Bells now. We're posting teams with spelling mistakes and scribbles on them – were the fundamentals of fantasy football the same, though, we wondered?

'Just like everyone else, I used to think I had the tactics nailed. GET THE STRIKER. He was first on the list. Goal-scoring midfielders next, decent goalkeeper, and then you'd be scrabbling about with 1.2 million left for a couple of shit defenders.' Yes. Yes, it was exactly the same! I mean, adjust the money for inflation, but other than that basic tactics don't change. Stop us when it starts sounding familiar. 'So, you'd go back and try to pinch a few million here and there – maybe not *the* best striker then, maybe one of the midfielders from one of the scrappy mid-table teams like Wimbledon, who, *yes*, did used to be Premier League, kids, and then go back to find you now had … 1.4 million for a couple of shit defenders.' As Homer Simpson would say, 'D'oh!', which would have still been an hilarious cultural reference back when Helen was playing fantasy football. Wet Wet Wet? Who remembers them?!

So, with the foolproof template, plus a knowledge of the beautiful game that puts the three of us flannels to shame (although, we'd like to add that we are old enough and knowledgeable enough to remember when Wimbledon played in the Premier League), was Helen actually any good at fantasy football? 'No.' Fair enough. Honesty is a good trait to have. To be fair, she could have lied. It's not like there's a career history that can be viewed and checked up on like the game today. But a little delve into Helen's fantasy footballing flaws does remind us of a particular stubborn Frenchman who resided in the red half of North London for a couple of decades: 'I never finished in a decent position in fantasy football, I was always crap at switching players. Funny how I'd be so obsessed at getting it right at the start, then couldn't be arsed to transfer anyone new, it used to be such a bloody palaver to do it – or maybe I was just convinced they'd all come good by the end of the season.' Yeah, Hells was doing Wenger before Wenger was doing Wenger. We can only assume she constantly came fourth in her mini-league every season and struggles with coat zips.

But, like Wenger, Helen had her favourites, and one of them in particular was the ultimate treasure for fantasy managers: 'A penalty-taking defender,' she swoons. 'Yeah, my best fantasy buy used to be Julian Dicks, I'd put him in first. A defender on penalties – what's not to love?' What's not to love about Julian Dicks, a notorious hard man of 90s football with a colourful disciplinary record, a fearsome reputation and a nickname of The Terminator? It's a good question, but certainly not one we're willing to answer in case we come across him at some kind of function in the future. He was bloody good at penalties, though.

Talking of coming across footballers, we wanted to know if, over the years of hosting *Soccer AM*, Helen had ever confronted one on letting her fantasy team down. Had she ever told one of the boys that they owed her four points for not keeping a clean sheet or getting sent off? 'I never held grudges against any players that didn't win me points, but I did used to thank the ones that had scored me an extra few, though.'

For anyone who has ever watched her on *Soccer AM* over the years – and let's face it, if you're a football fan and you haven't, then what are you watching from your living room floors on a Saturday morning? – you'll know that Helen is a colossal Torquay United fan. We enquired, hypothetically, if the Gulls were in the Premier League, would Helen be loyal and pick three of her own for her fantasy squad? 'OK, we may currently be top of the league at the time we're talking, but you do realise we are in the National League South, right? That's the *sixth tier* of English football. So, yes, I would definitely pick Torquay players in my fantasy team, but sadly I think the word "fantasy" is key here.' Quick, change the subject, she got angry. Loyal, but angry. Talk about darts!

Helen's into darts in a big way, and funnily enough fantasy football is one of the only hobbies in the world that is actually physically less demanding than a good game of arrows. We needed to know, as this book is all about the fantasy, who, in a fantasy scenario, would be better: Michael van Gerwen up front for Spurs or Harry Kane at the oche? She sided with Harry. 'A surprising amount of footballers can chuck a decent dart you know! Roger Johnson, ex Birmingham and Wolves, actually wanted to turn pro he was so good.' We're all just picturing Michael van Gerwen latching on to a cross from Dele Alli and nodding home the winner in a North London derby, aren't we?

We wanted to end our chat with the always spot-on Hells by asking what her go-to fantasy football team name was. As many of us know, and we have mentioned countless times already, a team name is a big factor. It doesn't have to be good, it doesn't have to be funny; in fact, it can be deliberately un-funny and shit, which in turn makes it funny. It will, however, largely revolve around a pun of some sort, so we decided to provide a couple of our own for Helen to use, just in case she decides to take up fantasy football again. The task was actually harder than we thought, and after 'Helen and the Chamberlain of Secret Points' and 'Torquay to Unlock any Defence' it did become a bit of a struggle. 'Thank you for your suggestions. Not gonna lie, they were, um, how do I put this politely? Gash.' Hurtful. 'I was always a bit rubbish at thinking up clever names for my teams as I just wanted to make sure "Torquay" was in them somewhere, in case I ended up near the top of the league, as I wanted to see their name in amongst the elite. I still think the most genius name for a team ever is the Sunday league side that play in Surrey called 'A3 Milan'. I never got near anything as good as that.' God, that's genius, get those lads a job writing jokes for us.

In our quest to cover all fantasy bases, we also wanted to know how the experts think. Sorry, we mean experts *other than ourselves*, of course, so we caught up with a couple of lads who are among the pioneers of fantasy football in the UK: Adam Jones and Andrew Butler of Dream Team FC. Our paths first crossed when both Andrew and our very own Craig were guests on TalkSPORT radio a few years ago to talk about – you'll never guess – fantasy bloody football, of all things. First thing's first, we thought, and asked Adam and Andrew if they are *actually* any good at fantasy football. Adam told us, 'I like to think I am, but perhaps dealing with statistics and tips all the time throws you off course a bit. Sometimes I think a little bit of ignorance can be bliss when making decisions.' On the subject of ignorance being bliss, Andrew added, 'One guy who won dream team weekender last year picked his team by auto-fill. Easiest cash he'll ever make.' There's ignorance being bliss and then there's making people like us – who are trying to make a career out of fantasy football chat and advice – redundant, when people can simply auto-fill their way to cash prizes. Jesus. That's where the pressure to not only be good at fantasy football, but give decent advice comes in. The burden to hand out at least a few genuinely good nuggets of information or tips, to keep your status as people who actually know what they're talking about intact. Personally, at The Gaffer Tapes, if we make mistakes or give someone a piece of advice that turns out to be particularly terrible, we maintain that we are a comedy outfit first and a fantasy football one second, thus covering our own occasionally incompetent (but hilarious) backs.

'A lot of the time it feels like we're preaching to the choir since the majority of our fanbase know what they're doing. I mean *really* know what they're doing', Adam says. 'There's all kinds of forums and wacky internet discussions crunching all the numbers.' It's an interesting point that, with so much fantasy football discussion and stats available to anyone with a computer or that's really, *really* good at smoke signals, maybe everyone's becoming an expert. Maybe the likes of The Gaffer Tapes and Dream Team FC will slip into obscurity as a result of fantasy football players becoming self-sufficient. Certainly, in the five years since we began broadcasting, at least 40 fantasy football podcasts have popped up out of nowhere. Some of them have even got in touch and thanked us for inspiring them to create their own fantasy football show, which is incredibly nice and we can only assume that the other fantasy football podcasts that *haven't* are too intimidated by our prowess, success and shiny award to get in touch. Bless.

The Dream Team lads acknowledge the responsibility of providing quality advice, seen as it is quite literally what they do. 'But yeah, obviously as tipsters we don't want to end up with egg on our face by telling everyone to ditch Harry Kane for Romelu Lukaku.' Incidentally, Lukaku can often be found with egg on *his* face, and his ever-expanding frame is testament to that.

As well as making the game into a genuine occupation, Adam and Andrew are players of fantasy football too, and there is, of course, a pretty competitive mini-league at Dream Team HQ. The boys tell us that they all stick a bit of money in the pot at the start of the season, meaning there's a cash prize for the individuals who finish first, second and third. There's also an obligatory wooden spoon prize for the unlucky soul who manages to finish last, as that is a pretty sizeable achievement in itself in the grand scheme of things.

When it comes to losing mini-leagues, running such a large fantasy football empire means they've also been privy to a punishment or two over the seasons. 'We've heard of some pretty outrageous forfeits down the years, but one poor guy who was forced to wear an Arsenal shirt to a Spurs game might take the biscuit.' I'm surprised that the Tottenham fans around him didn't ram said biscuit right up his Arse-nal shirt.

Andrew informs us that Premier League players love a bit of Dream Team too, although he also claims a piece of one of the most inspiring football stories of recent times as well. 'Jamie Vardy played Dream Team the season that Leicester won the Premier League, and we'd like to think that the motivation to score points was the reason behind his incredible form that season. Yeah, we've said it – we are the reason why Leicester won the Premier League.' You heard it here! Although, while we're all claiming stuff, I'd like to add that we want to take full credit for everything our adhesive namesake has done up to this point, including keeping Wayne Rooney's wig on his head. Vardy isn't the only pro getting involved – someone else who spends his weekend with one eye on his fantasy team is former Spurs midfielder Ryan Mason. 'He had a league on Dream Team in 2018/19 and he did alright – at the halfway point in the season he was in the top 100 in his league. It's nice to know that professional footballers are really just like us when it comes to fantasy football, it's a great leveller.' Coming in to contact with professional footballers who play fantasy football, particularly when it's through *your* format, throws up an interesting element. 'We've had a couple of players who play the game jokingly ask us whether or not we could fiddle around with a league, or Dream Team ratings, so that they'd get more points.' Scandal! Obviously, we wanted names (and email addresses so we can ask them to be guests on the podcast), but unfortunately Adam and Andrew maintained doctor-patient confidentiality. 'I can't name names,' Dr Andrew Butler MD tells us, 'but footballers are famously competitive and it even stretches to fantasy football.'

To be successful at the game, there probably does have to be a certain element of competitiveness, otherwise why else are we playing? For a laugh? Grow up, mate. Losers laugh, winners win … and also laugh, but they laugh once they've won. One of the downfalls of any fantasy football manager, even the big boys, is loyalty. If you have it, it can be a key factor in your demise and no amount of the aforementioned competitiveness can bring it back and save it for you.

Andrew's dependability has never been questioned whereas his sanity, however, is another sandwich for another picnic. But he claims that after all these seasons, he's beginning to learn his lesson. 'I'm overwhelmingly loyal to certain players, and it's to my detriment every single year. I never learn my lessons, mainly because I'm certain these players will come good once again. So, to Alex Song, Leighton Baines and Charlie Daniels I say thanks for the memories, but it's time to say goodbye for good.'

This loyalty is never more evident than in Andrew's unfaltering devotion to his beloved Leyton Orient. On the subject of a suggested non-league version of the game, that we thought would entice Andrew, he shot us down instantly, claiming there would be no need. 'I think you'll find Orient are going up this season, so I'd have no interest whatsoever in non-league fantasy football.' At the time of going to print, we have no idea as to whether Orient did in fact get promoted into the Football League – but let's be honest, it doesn't really matter. If they did, then congratulations to The Os and indeed to Mr Butler. If they didn't, then we'll have that conversation about Dream Team FC getting behind The Gaffer Tapes's non-league fantasy football empire next season.

We simply couldn't let Adam and Andrew go without asking the big, burning question, the one thing that fantasy football players and fans of the beautiful game alike wanted to know more than anything. More than the pressures and responsibility that comes with expertise, the inside workings of the game itself, the pitfalls and the question of undying loyalty, everyone really wants to know just how annoyed was everyone at Dream Team FC when The Gaffer Tapes beat them at the Football Blogging Awards at Old Trafford in 2016 when we scooped the Best Football Podcast Award? 'Absolutely farcical!' was the instant reply from Andrew, which was slightly hurtful if we're completely honest. 'We had James Buckley from *The Inbetweeners* hosting ours and we lost out to three guys talking about Fantasy Football. We even sent two lads up there to collect what was clearly rightfully ours and they came back into the office with nothing. They were both only 19 years old at the time and they cried for two days straight, so I hope you're proud of yourselves.' If there's one thing that you can say about us, it's that you can guarantee we are *always* pretty proud of ourselves, lads.

In 2012, star of BBC3's *The Luke McQueen Pilots*, a comedian aptly named Luke McQueen went viral when he posted a video on his YouTube channel of him standing outside the Emirates in a Tottenham shirt in a bid to prove his love to his ex-girlfriend Sarah and win her back. Sounds relatively traumatic and dangerous (Arsenal fans can be notoriously vicious with their selfie sticks) but what if we told you that Luke *is* an Arsenal fan. It is the first in a long line of pretty fearless stunts that Luke has pulled off both on TV and online. His BBC3 show saw him hijacking a live sex show in Amsterdam to perform a few jokes, and when that failed he got off with a sex doll onstage to the utter silent, abject horror of the live audience. A sex doll that Luke also, we must add, took around Amsterdam for a romantic day of sightseeing. So, we assumed that someone who is willing to dress up as a baby on national TV to test the mothering qualities of a group of horrified glamour models, and then shoot one of them with a paintball gun, would have some pretty shocking mini-league forfeits. 'There's always talk of stuff but nobody has the energy to bother. I think one year the bottom manager had to wear someone's mum's pants. I think he just kept them in his drawer for a year and allegedly never put them on. Now we just have the bottom half of the league paying for everyone's curry at the end of the season.'

Shifting the subject from pants of loyalty, we wondered where the allegiances would be of an Arsenal fan who has been seen by hundreds of thousands of people in a Spurs shirt standing outside his own team's ground, when it comes to the always controversial issue of picking rival players for his fantasy football team. 'I don't make a habit of it,' Luke said, 'I'm not one of those fans that bets against their club to hedge their bets. I can't take any consolation in Arsenal losing. When I did have Harry Kane at the club I made him train alone, I wanted him to know I didn't accept him in the same way I did the other lads.'

We'd like to put it out there and say that Luke McQueen is absolutely hilarious, and a particular video of his where he knocks on the front doors of unwitting members of the public and performs stand-up comedy to them on their doorstep is genuinely one of our favourite YouTube videos of all time. But the question is, is he as good at fantasy football as he is at making us laugh whilst sat in our pants on a

Tuesday afternoon or at performing gestures of unrequited love to Sarah? 'To answer this, I have to explain the type of format I'm restricted to. I'm in a league with normally around 10–12 other managers and nobody is allowed to have the same player. We don't use the draft system, instead we have an auction (often referred to as the "greatest day of the year") just before the season starts where we each have 100 million to bid on players; we then have an extra budget for transfers throughout the season where we make sealed bids through an outsider's email. This, to my knowledge so far, is the greatest way to play fantasy football.' Wow. A completely innovative, compelling take on playing fantasy football; I mean, he avoided the question of whether he is actually good, but excellent diversion. 'Am I good, did you say? There was a seven-year period where me and another manager came first and second, myself winning it three times. Also, I'm in a league with five Spurs fans and I managed to sign Harry Kane for 0.2 million during his first season. I always remind them that I knew Harry was going to be a top player before them; that's what top managers do, spot the talent early.'

With such a well-established mini-league and lofty stakes involving the underwear of mothers (good name for a progressive feminist rock band), we assumed Luke has seen some terrible fantasy football-related mistakes over the seasons. 'As I mentioned, we get a transfer budget for the season. One year a manager blew his entire budget on Balotelli. Unfortunately, you don't get any points for setting off some fireworks in your bathroom.' More's the pity. Can you imagine if you'd have activated your Bathroom Banger Chip that week?

We thought we'd end our chat with Luke – and our foray into the fantasy football teams of our well-known friends from the broad spectrum of sports and entertainment – by asking him our most hotly anticipated question. It's the one we'd been itching to ask the entire time; we'd left the best 'til last, we thought – what would such an hilarious, accomplished stand-up comedian call his fantasy football team? Ooh, this is going to be good. 'I always name my team "Sarah". If you're reading this, Sarah, please call me.'

Real Fans vs
Fantasy Fans

WATCHING your team play a game of football is incredibly cut-and-dried. You will, in all circumstances, want the side you support to score more goals than the opposition. Simple. We're not here to explain this most fundamental aspect of the game, but I feel that we did it pretty well. You should be requiring your team, let's call them 'Team A', to kick a ball into the goal more times than the opposition team, we'll dub 'Team B'. It's why the beautiful game has been around for so long, you know where you are – it really isn't rocket science. In fact, when you're watching a game, do you ever take a step back and really watch it? You know, take a look at what's actually happening on the field? Twenty-two men chasing a ball. I find that if I think about it too much my head hurts, it's a bit like trying to think about where the universe ends, or what happened to Darren Anderton. Football is, on face value, an unpretentious sport; it is easily explained, simple to follow and uncomplicated in its fundamentals. There could be a particular boxer you've always admired taking on an underdog you're quite keen on, and you feel torn. You can't decide who you want to win, and as the course of the pugilistic contest progresses, your allegiances may change several times. But this isn't two highly trained men putting their lives on the line and fighting for their families, for respect, in a battle of life and death, this is football. You should, at no point, feel any kind of conflict when watching your team of 11 overpaid men jogging around with 11 other equally overpaid men for hundreds of thousands of pounds. The only thing that I can think of that could complicate this incredibly simple ideology is fantasy football, 'the game of the beautiful game'.

I know someone who is so Everton through and through that not only will you never find him without an Everton shirt on, he'll be wearing an Everton waterproof training jacket, Everton jumper, Everton watch, Everton socks and if you pull down his Everton tracksuit bottoms – being careful that his Everton wallet doesn't fall out – you'll see a pair of Everton underpants. If you cut him, he'll yell 'ouch' in a scouse accent because he's an Evertonian. Interesting side-note: my spell checker is suggesting the word 'Evertonian' be changed to 'Everton Ian', which is definitely what I'll now be calling him, even though his name is actually Kevin.

Everton Ian is so loyal to the Toffees, so unrelentingly, staunchly Everton, that he refuses to include any player in his fantasy football team who wears red. As well as the whole 'ouch' thing, he also bleeds blue if you were to cut him, and his pure, unadulterated hatred for anything red is part of his commitment to the cause. As a result of his unfaltering morals, he's never picked a single Manchester United, Arsenal or, *of course*, Liverpool player in his fantasy team over the years, he hates Father Christmas and finds the process of posting a letter extremely difficult. His side will instead be made up of players wearing blue; obviously it will include the full three Everton players, a handful of Chelsea and some Man City (although it's technically the wrong shade of blue), but after that it does become a little trickier to assemble a well-rounded, successful fantasy squad. He allows himself a Tottenham player or two, because of the navy shorts, but the likes of Bournemouth, Watford and West Ham are all complete no-nos, and Crystal Palace in their half blue-half red shirt? Are you kidding, mate? Needless to say, Everton Ian is shit at fantasy football. Incredibly shit. Like, the shittest. He'll hold his hands up and admit it, although he'll do it slowly so his Everton sweatbands and matching signet ring don't fly off. Everton Ian doesn't care, though, because Everton Ian is an Everton fan first, and a fantasy football fan second. Some, however, don't show the same loyalty.

I myself wrestled with my conscience and loyalty in the early days of fantasy football. Could I bring myself to add a Spurs player to my side as a lifelong Gooner? Would I be able to sleep at night and look at myself in the mirror when I woke, knowing I'd sold out, made the cardinal sin and welcomed the mortal enemy into my ranks. Then there was a season where Gareth Bale was mis-classified – and therefore mispriced – as a defender, and I thought, 'Ah, fuck it'. Since then, I have betrayed my beloved Arsenal many times a season, whether it's been with Robbie Keane, Jermain Defoe, Dele Alli or Harry Kane, I've accepted them all into my red-and-white bosom. There are many like me. Millions of fantasy football players leave their loyalty at the door when it comes to picking their team. If you want to be successful and have a shot at beating your mates who don't give a toss if they're a United fan or not when they're captaining Sergio Agüero, then you have to essentially become an absolute Judas as well. There's also the way of thinking, for some, that a loss for your team against their greatest rival can be somewhat softened if you've included some of the opposition players in your fantasy team. 'Yeah, it was horrible to see my Arsenal lose a North London derby, but I captained Kane, so it's not all bad.' [Disclaimer: if you have ever said this or anything that could be even construed as similar then I hate every single fibre of you, including the fibres of your half-and-half scarf.]

What is more important at the end of the day: that your team wins in a real game of football, or that *you* win at a fake game? However you answer this question reveals the type of fantasy football manager you are and – more tellingly – what sort of a football fan you are. Are you an *Everton Ian* or a *Half-and-Half Henry*?

Supporting *your* team, following *your* side is the biggest part of football. Personally, if someone doesn't know who their team is playing at the weekend when asked, I don't class them as a true fan. Equally, I wouldn't class someone as a true fan if they are one of the increasing amount of people who seem to hate their rivals more than they love their team – the kind of fan I am seeing all too often on social media who celebrates their arch-enemy's loss far more than their own club's win. I'm not pointing to any particular fan base – *especially* not Scotland fans after England's World Cup 2018 semi-final exit – but it is absolutely rife on the toxic cesspool that is sites such as Twitter. The term 'troll' is wildly overused nowadays, but you can understand how the moniker came about by the way these creepy little keyboard-warriors/smartphone-commandos tend to crawl, unprovoked, from their particular hole on to timelines to spout abuse towards a rival team with such ferocious venom that it genuinely does make me fear for the human race a little bit. The United fans who are itching to rub Liverpool's face in any loss and remind the fans how much they've won in the last two decades compared to them. The Arsenal supporters who laugh at Spurs when they get knocked out of any competition and tweet a picture of an empty trophy cabinet complete with cobwebs. The Spurs fans who laugh right back at Arsenal when they finish above them for the season and remind the Gunners that it's actually been a very long time since they won the league. Then there's Rangers and Celtic fans … best leave that there, maybe. These weird, spiteful little goblins trawl through social media just looking for someone to attack, someone who may have been celebrating their team being one-nil up an hour ago, to then rub their faces in the fact that they ended up losing. It's the unsolicited nature of invading someone's personal cyberspace and having a go at them for something they like. You wouldn't do that in real life, would you? Imagine standing outside Subway waiting for people to come out with a big beef melt before yelling in their faces repeatedly that big beef melts are shit and they are fucking idiots for buying them. It also often dawns on me that these obsessives spend the hours of 3pm to 4.45pm relentlessly goading people foolish enough to have their football allegiances in their Twitter bio so therefore they can't be watching any actual football. Like getting involved in heated and hate-filled debates on an *Eastenders* forum when you don't even watch it, just read the blurb in the TV guide every day while claiming you're a diehard 'Ender. The thing is, I would put money on the fact that a lot of these trolls, who spout so much hatred and bile about their rival team and their fans, will have a player or two from said team in their fantasy football squad. If you want to be half-decent at fantasy football, you can't be overly loyal, or you simply won't be making the most of your opportunities; if you're putting any kind of restrictions on yourself then you're not playing the game to its full capacity and you won't be reaping the rewards. You'll be loyal alright, you'll be able to brag that you hate your rivals so much that you can't even bring yourself to put one of them in your fantasy football team, but you'll be bragging from the lower half of your mini-league, pal. Loyalty can be overrated.

A former colleague of mine was a Tottenham fan (hence why I firmly class him as a 'colleague' and not a 'friend'), and he used to bet against Spurs so that if they lost the cash he'd win would soften the blow. Once again, you would question the loyalty and integrity of someone who bets against their own team, but he was certainly the Spurs fan first, who was always genuinely gutted when they lost, and the 'better' second. Some, like Everton Ian, wouldn't wager a single penny against their team in a million years. Some *would* bet against their team but take no real enjoyment in picking up their winnings knowing their boys lost. Some, however, would take more enjoyment from receiving their tainted monies when their team lose than the joy of when they win. It's an absolute minefield of morals and people navigate it in very different ways. Personally, I don't think I would have a problem with betting against Arsenal. I've certainly never done it, but that's more down to the fact that I am petrified of bookies, or more specifically *the bigger boys* in bookies, and less to do with any ethical reasoning. I can understand how it would take the edge off a loss, but it would worry me that on a particularly tough financial month, maybe just after Christmas or just after the release of the *even bigger* beef melt, I would find a small part of myself actually wishing my team lost. If I was strapped for cash, the thought of a few quid might seem more appealing than three points. I wouldn't want to juggle those conflicting emotions, so I won't put myself in that potentially difficult situation. I wouldn't want to be watching Arsenal 1-0 down to Chelsea, two minutes of injury time left to play, Arsenal breaking, on what must be the final attack of the game, praying they don't score so I can pick up a much needed 40 notes. That very plausible situation is why I would never bet against my team. Plus, have you seen the fellas in the bookies? Some of them haven't got any teeth!

If you had to ask someone who doesn't know much about football what a football fan looked like, they would probably use the words 'scarf', 'skinhead' and/or 'Burberry'. Obviously, we know this isn't the case. Equally, if you asked someone who doesn't know much about *fantasy* football what a fantasy football player looks like, I'm pretty sure 'spectacles', 'laptop' and 'still lives at home with his mum' would crop up. Again, we know this is far from the case – most of the time. Yes, some football fans like to throw on a bit of Stone Island, tuck their tracksuit bottoms into their socks, drink 12 pints and throw up in the away stand, but let's not forget that a lot of those undesirables will also have a fantasy football team. Equally, the little fella in his bedroom with his glasses, laptop and spreadsheets will sit and watch every single televised game, including streaming all the non-televised games, proving himself to be more of a football fan than the geezer going up to Chelsea just to get twatted, who wakes up the next morning with a black eye and no idea what the final score was.

A pretty decent percentage of football fans are fantasy football players, but a much higher percentage of fantasy football players are football fans. Technically, you *can* play fantasy football and not be a fan of the actual game of football, but you're unlikely to be overly successful and sure to become very bored incredibly quickly. You don't have to support a particular club; in fact, I know several fantasy football players who don't follow anyone anymore, but watch enough football to get by. In fact, you will probably find that if you don't support a Premier League team, or don't have any allegiances to any football club in particular, you may be a better fantasy football manager than someone who follows a team directly involved in fantasy football. But whether you support a Premier League side or not, as long as you play fantasy football, it will change how you watch football for good. There's the potential for you to have an interest in every single top-flight game that weekend. Burnley vs Brighton on a wet Monday night becomes as exciting as El Clásico, mate. Midweek fixture between Newcastle and Everton? It's like the bloody World Cup Final to me; I've got three players taking part, including my captain. If you've got something riding on it, even if it's just the one player, it makes that game interesting. You'll find yourself praying for a boring 0-0 when Crystal Palace take on Southampton in the Friday night kick-off that no one is watching, because you've got a defender from both teams in your starting line-up. People at the pub will think you're absolutely mental when you're cheering every wayward pass and shot that goes miles wide, but that's 12 fantasy points right there.

You'll find yourself interested in how the second-choice Wolves left-back is playing as you're watching them host Watford on an illegal stream on your phone, while

Liverpool take on Chelsea on the two giant screens in the pub. Your non-fantasy playing mates will think you've either lost the plot or you're just a huge enthusiast who doesn't discriminate between matches and believes that all games of football are as beautiful as each other. But you can't enjoy Mo Salah, Marcos Alonso and Roberto Firmino as they put on a masterclass in HD, as you're too busy squinting at the moody footage from Molineux on your six-inch screen, hoping your punt on the young Wolves lad pays off. This is because, sadly, as well as fantasy football *changing* the way you watch football, it can also *ruin* the way you watch football.

It's very rare that in this age of everyone having a device with access to the internet in their pockets we wouldn't know the football scores unless we watched the classified results being read out on the BBC. The iconic voice of the late, great Tim Gudgin, an absolute British institution, was the only way you would know the full football results back in the day. You wouldn't be able to celebrate or commiserate until the official classified results had come from Gudgin's lips. There was an air of finality to it, you trusted him, and unless Tim Gudgin had said it, it wasn't gospel, it simply wasn't over. This primary platform for the football scores was broadened in the 90s by the addition of teletext. I can't tell you the number of afternoons I spent round a mate's house in front of the black screen, watching the turquoise, white and luminous yellow writing, waiting for an update. If we were bowling around town in our Adidas Popper tracksuit bottoms and Reebok Classics, we would always stop off in Dixons and use the teletext on the TVs in there to check the scores. We'd then do a lap of the town, sit in McDonald's for ten minutes around one small coke, so they *technically* couldn't throw us out, then head back to Dixons again for another update, before calling Mum on a payphone to ask what time dinner was ready. Ah, they really were simpler times.

At no point was there ever anything overly complicated going on. I'd want Arsenal to win, Dave wanted West Ham and Sharpy liked rugby. Simple. I always wanted Man United to lose because, even at the age of 12 or 13, the idea that these lads at school who were born and grew up in the south-east of England supported a team from up north just because they won all the time was incredibly annoying. In fact, I still use the same response I used back then on hearing someone is a United fan: 'What part of Manchester are you from?' God, that used to annoy people. No wonder I only had two friends. Other than constantly yearning for the demise of Manchester United, which, let's be honest, very rarely happened back in the 90s, I wouldn't really care about the other results. After I'd seen how Arsenal were getting on, Dave had checked West Ham and Sharpy had moaned about footballers being pussies, I'd scan the other results but ultimately forget them, so that by the time I was watching *Match of the Day* that evening I could enjoy watching the highlights not knowing the results. But those were the days before I played fantasy football ...

The constant checking of every result, of who's been booked, how many that team have conceded, whether that player has played enough minutes. You're invested in almost every aspect of every game. It's not just the results and stats of the games that the players in your fantasy team are playing in, but the results and stats of the players who have been picked by your closest rivals in your mini-league. If you're serious about your fantasy football, then it's very rare that a game will go by without any implications whatsoever for you. As a result of this, you're checking everything. Luckily, nowadays you have access to every kind of stat you need on your smartphone or laptop; you can check everything you need to know. Football matches aren't matches played on a football field any more, they're a list of numbers that either hurt you or help you, and this is how you will view football now. Gone are the days of playing the '*Match of the Day* Challenge', where you don't know the scores before watching, where you deliberately avoid watching *Final Score*, and you turn away when the newsreader tells you to so you don't see the scores when they flash up on *The Ten O'clock News*. There's probably no need to watch *Match of the Day* at all nowadays, you'll know every kick of the ball and every significant minute of the game just by the match reports and stats that you've been pouring over for the majority of the day, trying to understand why Josh King didn't get higher ranked in the bonus point system.

You *will*, of course, watch *Match of the Day*, however, but not through the eyes of your younger self who was brimming with excitement and enthusiasm at the prospect of watching highlights from the day's games, when anything was possible. But watching it through the jaded, cynical eyes of a man who knows too much and has seen more than his fair share of heartache at the hands – or rather *feet* – of football for that day. You don't want to be reminded of how badly you have done, and even if you had a good fantasy football day there's every chance you're sick of the sight of it all by 10.35pm of a Saturday night, even though technically you have watched very little actual football. You've simply collected your points and now want to sit down and forget about football for a bit. It's as if it's a real job. If you were a real football manager, you probably wouldn't want to sit down in front of *Match of the Day* and watch everyone else. It's a bit of a busman's holiday.

I'd like to organise an event where all your mates in your mini-league get together, maybe in the back room of a pub or in your richest mate's front room, and you all watch *Match of the Day,* having no idea of the day's scores. Phones are turned off and left by the front door, and you sit and watch, for the first time, as the day's football unfolds. Imagine the excitement again, the electricity of not knowing, the endless possibility. Not only are you watching as a football fan and follower of your team, but as a fantasy football manager. You'll be staying glued to that TV until the often maligned last game. While phones are strictly forbidden, paper and pens are permitted, no *encouraged,* as you attempt to work out your fantasy points as you go along. You'll be watching everything, every flash at the bottom about yellow cards, scrutinising every assist to see if it was your boy, working out if your captain is likely to be awarded bonus points, or did he not get around the pitch enough?

Then, once everything is done, you've all watched and enjoyed the highlights of every game and have a scruffy piece of paper with an educated guess at what your fantasy football score for that day might be, it's finally time to check. Could I suggest that maybe instead of everyone turning on their individual phones to check their fantasy scores, maybe you hook up a laptop to the TV screen to have a look at your mini-league? I mean, granted, it's extra work, but the big reveal will be a hell of a lot more rewarding. One screen with everything on it that you need to know, instantly uncovered with the click of a button. I can hear the groans and cheers reverberating around the room already. Then there's the potential for an additional season-long game where you keep a count of whose predicted score is closest to their actual score each week, and run a league table. Oh my god, I'm getting excited!

What a way to bring the innocent, long-lost excitement and enthusiasm back to football and, to a further extent, fantasy football. To me, a person who swims in a sea of nostalgia on a day-to-day basis and misses Teletext and Manchester United fans born in the Royal Borough of Windsor & Maidenhead (they're all City fans now), **The *Match of the Day* Fantasy Challenge**™ is something I think we should all try. Add another layer of magic to football and fantasy football alike. Bring the fun back. Don't drown in stats and figures and worry about points all day long, bring it back to grass roots. It's easy to forget that football is a game you love, when you get too bogged down in ranks and the bonus point system. In short, don't let fantasy football ruin how you watch football, let it add to it. Enjoy it in conjunction with the real game. Live it and breathe it as it happens. Well, several hours later and heavily edited, but you know what I mean.

Personally, I think **The *Match of the Day* Fantasy Challenge**™ is quite easily the best idea I've ever had and I've just suggested it to my mini-league WhatsApp group. Dave's up for it, but Sharpy called us a couple of pussies.

Death, Taxes and Fantasy Football

S O that's it. We've guided you through the murky underworld that is fantasy football. If you didn't enjoy it or don't feel like you gained what you had hoped, then please do read it again. We wrote it in such a way that you will unearth layered gems you didn't catch the first time round. If you've now done that and still don't feel that you learnt as much as you had hoped, then please don't read it a third time. It just probably isn't for you and we are sorry we wasted your time. Before you re-gift us to a friend or donate us to a charity shop, though, have you ever considered sneaking us back into the book shop you bought us from? Slyly pop us back on the shelves and then someone else has to pay full price just like you did. Everyone's a winner! Except the charity shop. We forgot about them.

I recently cleared out my teenage bedroom from my parents' house and among the Lynx shower gel gift sets and

Kickers jumpers I found a plethora of books that had been bought for me over the years by my grandmother. A book is a classic Christmas go-to for the not-so-sure nan, and mine would often gift me one based on something I might have mentioned in passing once whilst dropping her off at bingo. She really is a cliché nan, isn't she? They're the best kind. However, it means that if I mentioned Jamie Carragher's revival under Brendan Rodgers to my dad then I can expect *Carra: My Autobiography* under the tree come December. One of the books I found among the sea of ghost-written footballer memoirs was Frank Skinner's autobiography. He wasn't someone I mentioned in passing on a car journey to feed an elderly woman's gambling addiction. Ever since I saw him talk about football on a sofa in a way that no one else on TV did or could, I was fascinated by him. He put a non-athletic face on football, he made fantasy football cool and he made an 11-year-old me realise that I wanted to be just like him, just without the alcoholism and Catholicism. I read that book three or four times and when I found it clearing out that bedroom, in the midst of writing this book, I read it again. It's still the same incredible book it was over 15 years ago. Next to it on the dusty bookshelf was Justin Lee Collins's *Good Times*! That's the thing with my nan, she was very hit and miss. Not something Justin ever did if the reports are to be believed. We hope that in years to come you find this and look upon it without regret. That it reminds you of your hours agonising over team selection and reminiscing about how simple the game used to be now that you have 73 chips and Brexit has banned anyone not called John playing football in Britain. We hope that it sits on the Frank Skinner side of the fence and conjures fond memories and not tales of having to log sexual encounters and sleep facing your spouse or risk being berated. Justin didn't include those bits in the book FYI.

If nothing else, this book will have opened your eyes to the depths of obsession that exists within the game we all love. If fantasy football hasn't led to you running marathons with no training, missing the birth of your child or stealing your friend's wife then things aren't that bad. You can reassure your husband or wife that it could get much, much worse. Make it sound like a threat. And let's be honest, they are going to need to learn to live with it just like we have because, and I can't stress this enough, it's not going anywhere. Fantasy football can't be put back in the box. We've gone too far. People have tattoos! Whether you use this book as a way to up the ante with your mates or heed it as a word of warning for how things can get out of hand is up to you. But, if you get asked to join a Heung-Min Son league next year then don't come crying to us when you find out the person who loses has to join the army. We tried to tell you.

Whether the future of football turns out like an episode of *The Hurricanes* or 22 Jesse Lingards running around, phone in hand, streaming their game on their insta story, there will be a group of friends somewhere counting points for clean sheets, assists and hover-goals. It's the future, remember. And, if in the future an alien *does* read this book on a quest to learn about 'the game of the beautiful game', as we pondered in the introduction, then hopefully the little fella will take a better understanding of it back to his home planet. Will he know how to become a universal fantasy footballing overlord and rule the entire galaxy with his infinite knowledge of differentials, bonus point distribution and algorithms? No. Will he know the best ways to get into his little alien mates' heads to drive them mental all season? Yeah. Yeah, we think he will. Because all fantasy football players are aliens really. We're not like the 'normal' people. We talk a different language and float around, vacantly pointing at things of interest and wanting to understand them better, the quest for knowledge, power and supremacy at the forefront of our supremely advanced brains. We spend too much time in cyberspace, and we have all wanted to phone home after a bad game week. Maybe fantasy football players *are* an extraterrestrial race and we were sent to earth to take over. If that is the case, then this book is our bible. Our holy scripture on how we should treat others and live our lives ... or we're all just nerds with spreadsheets.